*100 great recipes*

# Vegetarian

# 100 great recipes

# Vegetarian

Vicki Smallwood

Published by SILVERDALE BOOKS
An imprint of Bookmart Ltd
Registered number 2372865
Trading as Bookmart Ltd
Blaby Road
Wigston
Leicester LE18 4SE

D&S Books Ltd
Kerswell,
Parkham Ash, Bideford
Devon, England
EX39 5PR

e-mail us at:-
enquiries@d-sbooks.co.uk

This edition printed 2005

ISBN 1-84509-186-8

DS0121. 100 Great Vegetarian Recipes

Creative Director: Sarah King
Editor: Clare Haworth-Maden
Project editor: Sally MacEachern
Designer: Debbie Fisher
Photographer: Colin Bowling/Paul Forrester

Fonts: New York, Helvetica and Bradley Hand

Printed in China

1 3 5 7 9 10 8 6 4 2

# Contents

# introduction

A vegetarian diet does not have to be dull, brown, bland or boring, as I hope this book will show you. Vegetarians are just like other people who want a varied and tasty diet, the only difference being that they do not want to eat meat or any of its by-products. This is easily done when you know how, and today's market caters for vegetarians more than ever before. Years ago, vegetarian foods were only readily available from health-food shops, but thankfully today's supermarkets and even smaller shops have realised that there is an ever-growing demand for vegetarian foods that needs to be tapped into and catered for. Even huge fast-food chains that were previously famous for their meat-based menus are adding vegetarian options to their ranges, which can only be due to public demand. In short, vegetarianism is becoming more widespread and is clearly no longer considered a fad or a passing phase exhibited by a minority of people.

In the past, however, a vegetarian diet was thought of by some people as being a little odd. This was due partly to ignorance and partly to the media. For example, Neil, a character in *The Young Ones*, a popular British comedy series of the 1980s, was portrayed as a vegetarian student who was a little slow, the butt of most people's jokes and living on huge vats of lentils that were made to look as unappetising as possible.

Perhaps needless to say, for a long time, people generally thought that a vegetarian diet meant lentils, beans, nut loaf and all that results from eating them! Yet these foods can all be very appetising if cooked in the right way, and thankfully attitudes towards vegetarians are changing. This is probably due in no small part to some of the horrendous stories that have been reported in the media in recent years regarding the treatment of livestock, meat and its by-products.

Today, more and more people are eating less meat by choice. Indeed, surveys show that sections of the population are often voluntarily eating meals that contain no meat, even though they are not vegetarian. Meat-eating people sometimes think that a meal is not a meal unless it has meat in it, but if you ask a meat-eater to cast his or her mind back over the last week, they will no doubt be surprised to remember at least one meal that they have eaten and enjoyed that did not include meat. If, for instance, you had a bag of chips that hadn't been fried in animal fat on the way home, then that was a vegetarian meal (admittedly not a healthy one, but a vegetarian one all the same).

I hope that this book will cater for meat-eaters and vegetarians alike. If, for instance, you enjoy meat, but are beginning to think about reducing the amount that you eat, then this book should be of help to you. And if you are starting to experiment with vegetarianism, or a family member is a vegetarian, then I am sure that it will be useful because it contains many dishes that can be enjoyed in a household whose members follow both a vegetarian diet and a meat-based diet. There are lots of dishes in here that will please all sorts of tastes.

I sometimes find that it is better not to mention the addition or lack of a certain ingredient, i.e. meat, in a dish and instead just to sit back and wait to see if it is even noticed. There have been many occasions on which I have served up a totally vegetarian meal, whether it be home-cooked or an Indian takeaway, for example, without mentioning to the meat-eaters that it contains no meat. The result, I have found, has always been the same: empty plates and satisfied sighs. This goes to show that the lack of meat may not be missed if you don't point it out. However, I am pretty certain that there would have been a few murmurs of disapproval if, at the start of the meal, the meat-eaters had thought that because meat wasn't on the menu, the meal would be lacking in flavour or that they somehow wouldn't enjoy it.

There are many excellent meat substitutes on the market, so if you think that you will miss burgers, bacon and sausages, take a look at the vegetarian section of your supermarket or health-food shop and try out one of the many alternatives that you'll find there. I am sure that you have read, or heard, about the highly dubious ingredients or body parts that go into some processed meat products, but buy a vegetarian alternative, and you won't have to worry about what it contains.

The Vegetarian Society provides a wealth of information. In what follows I have relied heavily on material from their website (www.vegsoc.org).

# Different types of vegetarian

There are 3 million vegetarians in the UK, and in a recent poll it was shown that many other people are now eating no red meat, are eating only fish or are eating at least one vegetarian meal a week, so that they are all reducing their consumption of meat. There are many different types of vegetarian, and statistics show that increasing numbers of people are becoming more open to the concept of eating meals that don't contain meat or, at the very least, contain less meat.

## The vegetarian categories are as follows:

- The most common type of vegetarian is a lacto-ovo-vegetarian, or a vegetarian who eats dairy products and eggs.

- A lacto-vegetarian is a vegetarian who eats dairy products, but not eggs.

- There is also a growing group of people who are opting for a demi-veg diet, which means that they choose to eat little or no meat, but may eat fish.

- Vegetarians who eat only fish are sometimes called pescetarians.

- A vegan is a vegetarian whose diet does not contain dairy products or eggs, or, indeed, any animal products.

- A less common type is the fruitarian. A fruitarian diet is similar to a vegan diet: it contains mainly raw fruit, nuts and grains, with very few processed or cooked foods. Fruitarians believe that their diet should consist only of foods that can be harvested without killing a plant.

- Finally, there is the macrobiotic diet, which is probably the most extreme because it progresses through different levels, each one aimed at achieving a balance between the Chinese concepts known as yin and yang. Not all levels are vegetarian, but each one works towards eliminating animal products from the diet. At the highest level – the brown-rice diet – even fruits and vegetables have been eliminated.

This book caters for the most common of these vegetarian groups: the lacto-ovo-vegetarian one.

# A well-balanced
## vegetarian diet

When you are no longer including meat or fish in your diet, you will need to make sure that you eat other foods that supply the same nutrients. This is actually not too difficult, and in any case, a lot of people would do well to think a little more carefully about what they eat! All of your nutritional requirements can be easily obtained from a well-balanced vegetarian diet, and research has, in fact, proved that a vegetarian diet is far healthier than that of a meat-eater. Medical research has shown, for example, that a lifelong vegetarian will go to hospital on average 22 per cent less than a meat-eater, and a study conducted by Oxford University has concluded that vegetarians are 40 per cent less likely to be stricken by certain forms of cancer, and are also 50 per cent less likely to suffer from gallstones.

# Protein sources

Meat gives us protein, fat and some B vitamins and minerals, mostly iron and zinc. Fish supplies the same nutrients, but with the addition of vitamins A, D and F. To start with, many people worry about where they will get their daily requirement of protein from when they are no longer eating meat and fish. The answer is that nuts (like almonds, brazil nuts, cashews, hazelnuts, pine kernels and walnuts), seeds (including linseeds, pumpkin, sesame and sunflower seeds), pulses (such as beans, peas, peanuts and lentils), grains and cereals (barley, maize, or sweet corn, millet, oats, rice, rye and wheat, for example), soya products (for instance, tempeh, textured soya protein, tofu, soya milk and vegetable protein), dairy products (including cheese, milk and yoghurt) and eggs are not only all excellent sources of protein, but easy to include in a daily diet.

Women need approximately 45g of protein a day, a requirement that increases if they are leading a very active life, or are pregnant or breast-feeding. Men generally need approximately 55g, but require more if they are very active. Most people eat more protein than they need each day.

# Fat sources

Fats and oils receive a bad press, but are an essential part of a balanced diet. They are necessary for the manufacture of hormones within the body, act as carriers for some vitamins and also keep our tissues in good repair. The important thing to remember is that you should eat the right sorts of fats and oils, and then not to excess. Fats are either saturated or non-saturated, and non-saturated fats are either mono-unsaturated or poly-unsaturated. Animal fats tend to be saturated, and a high intake of these can lead to raised blood cholesterol. Vegetable fats are generally unsaturated.

# Carbohydrate sources

Our main, and most important, source of energy is carbohydrates, which are primarily provided by plant foods. There are three main types of carbohydrates: simple sugars, complex carbohydrates (or starches) and dietary fibre.

Simple sugars are found in fruit, milk and ordinary sugar. It is not good to include refined sources of sugar in your diet because they provide no fibre, vitamins or minerals and are the main cause of dental decay.

Complex carbohydrates are now known to be positively beneficial to our health, and should not be avoided, as was previously recommended by some people in the past. Complex carbohydrates are found in bread, pasta, rice, barley, millet, buckwheat and rye. The more unrefined complex carbohydrates you eat, the better because they will also supply you with essential dietary fibre and B vitamins. A diet that consists of 50 to 70 per cent complex carbohydrates is recommended by the World Health Organisation (WHO).

Dietary fibre is today called non-starch polysaccharide (NSF). This is the non-digestible part of a carbohydrate food. Wholegrain, or unrefined, foods are high in NSF, as are fruits, both fresh and dried, and vegetables. Ensuring that you eat plenty of NSF is now known to be a good safeguard against succumbing to many digestive ailments, and can even help to protect you from developing cancer of the colon. The government is constantly telling us that we should eat five portions of fruit and/or vegetables a day, and by following that piece of advice, we would be gaining valuable NSF, along with the vitamins and minerals that fruits and vegetables contain. This target is much easier to meet than you may at first imagine when you consider that a portion is the equivalent of as little as one apple, a small bunch of grapes or a handful of dried fruit.

# vitamin and
# mineral sources

Vitamins, which cannot be synthesised by the body, are needed each day, but in relatively small quantities. The vitamin that is present in virtually all meat, yet not in cereals, nuts, pulses, fruits and most vegetables, is B12. This can be a cause for concern for some vegetarians, but if you eat cheese and free-range eggs and drink milk, there is really nothing to worry about because you will be gaining vitamin B12 from these foods. Nowadays, B12 is also often added to some breakfast cereals, soya milk, bread, veggie burgers and yeast extracts, too.

Here is an outline of which foods contain which vitamins:

- Vitamin A is found in dairy produce and is added to most margarines; it is also present in leafy, green vegetables and in red, orange and yellow vegetables.

- B vitamins (apart from B12, see above) are found in yeast, wholegrain cereals wheat germ, nuts, pulses, seeds and green vegetables.

- Fresh fruits contain vitamin C, and particularly citrus fruits, salad vegetables, leafy, green vegetables and potatoes (new potatoes have a higher vitamin-C content than old potatoes).

- Vitamin D is made in the body as a result of being exposed to sunlight, and is not found in plant foods. It is added to most margarines and is present in milk, cheese and butter. It can be stored within the body, so as long as you eat at least one good portion of such foods a week, that should be ample.

- Vitamin E is gained by eating free-range eggs, wholegrain cereals, wheat germ and vegetable oil.

- Vitamin K is found in fresh vegetables and cereals, and can also be produced by bacteria in the intestines.

Minerals are also a daily requirement for the maintenance of a healthy body.

- Calcium is important for the bones and teeth. Young and old people need slightly more calcium than average, and must also have vitamin D because this helps the body to absorb calcium. Calcium is found in dairy produce, leafy, green vegetables, bread, nuts, seeds and dried fruits. Hard water is also a good source of this mineral.

- Iron is essential for the production of red blood cells. Women, and particularly young girls, need slightly more iron in their diet than average. Note that vitamin C assists the body's absorption of iron. Leafy, green vegetables, wholemeal bread, molasses, eggs, dried fruits, lentils and other pulses are all good sources of iron.

- Zinc is crucial for a well-functioning immune system and many enzyme reactions. Wholegrain cereals, green vegetables, cheese, sesame seeds, pumpkin seeds and lentils all supply us with zinc.

# Putting it all together

The breakdown of our nutritional requirements as outlined may sound complicated, but all that it really boils down to is that we must eat a balanced vegetarian diet each day in order to stay healthy. This means that every day we must eat a little oil or fat, some milk, cheese, free-range eggs or soya products, plus some nuts, seeds or pulses or beans, at least five portions of fruit and vegetables, as well as some bread, cereal, rice or pasta. Now, that doesn't sound quite so difficult, does it?

And it becomes even easier when you look at the lists of protein, carbohydrate, fat, vitamin and mineral sources above and think of them more as ingredients of meals than lists of food groups. A single day's example of a well-balanced vegetarian diet could comprise, for instance, muesli with dried fruits and nuts or wholemeal toast and a fruit yoghurt for breakfast; a noodle salad or a toasted sandwich and a piece of fruit for lunch; a vegetable curry with brown rice or a pie and vegetables, or even pasta with sauce and cheese for supper; along with snacks of fresh or dried fruit, vegetables, bread, nuts or seeds during the day. Think of food groups as potential meals in this way, and following a well-balanced diet seems easily achievable.

# Ingredients to avoid

Try to avoid eating a lot of processed food, which is not only nutritionally less good for you than fresh food, but may also contain hidden ingredients that are incompatible with a vegetarian diet.

The list below gives you an indication of some ingredients to look out for and steer clear of.

- Animal fats are generally carcass fats, and are not derived from milk.

- Aspic is a savoury jelly made from meat or fish.

- Biscuits are often made with animal fat.

- Caviar is obtained by killing fish to harvest their eggs (the caviar).

- Cheese has often had animal rennet (see below) added to it. Many cheeses made using the vegetarian alternative to rennet are now available (look for the Vegetarian Society's symbol on the label).

- Chocolate can contain whey (see below) and emulsifiers that may not be vegetarian.

- Cochineal, which may be identified on a food label as E120, is a colouring made from crushed insects.

- On a food label, edible fats is a rather vague and misleading description that can actually mean animal fats.

- When it comes to eggs, it is best always to eat free-range or organic ones.

- Gelatine, which is used in many sweets and jellies, is made from animal bones, skins, tendons, ligaments and so on. There are, however, vegetarian alternatives, such as agar agar, carrageen and gelozone.

- Glycerine can be produced from animal fats.

- Check an ice cream's label to ensure that it does not contain animal fats.

- Jelly generally contains gelatine (see above).

- Margarines can sometimes contain animal fats, fish oils and even gelatine (see above).

- Pastries sometimes have animal fats in them.

- Pepsin is an enzyme taken from a pig's stomach that is used like rennet (see below).

- Rennet is an enzyme extracted from the stomach of a newly killed calf and is widely used in the cheese-making process. Cheese can, however, be made using a vegetarian alternative. Such cheeses are generally clearly labelled with a vegetarian symbol.

- Roe, like caviar, is actually fish eggs that are obtained by killing fish.

- Soap is often made using animal fats and/or glycerine (see above). Many vegetable-oil soaps are available nowadays, however.

- Ready-made soups may have been prepared with animal stock, so check the label to ensure that vegetable stock was used.

- Suet is generally made from animal fat, but there are now several brands of vegetable suet on the market that are suitable for a vegetarian diet.

- Sweets can contain either gelatine or cochineal (see above for further information on both), so check the label to see whether these ingredients are listed.

- Toothpaste may contain glycerine, but health-food shops and large supermarkets often stock different brands that are suitable for a vegetarian diet.

- Washing powder that is soap-based may contain animal fats.

- Whey and whey powder are usually by-products of the cheese-making process and may consequently contain animal rennet (see above).

- Worcestershire sauce generally contains anchovies (small fish); a vegetarian variety is now available, so check the label before buying a bottle.

- Yoghurts – usually low-fat ones – may contain gelatine (see above), so check the label.

The basic rule is that if you aren't sure what a product contains, read the label.

# Enjoy!

I have tried to include lots of different styles of cooking, along with some old favourites and versions of newer dishes, among the recipes in this book. There are dishes to satisfy most tastes, as well as a range of dishes to suit most occasions. The methods advocated are not too challenging, and even the novice cook should be able to prepare a wide range of the recipes that appear in the following pages.

I hope that this book will give you pleasure, and will perhaps go some way in showing meat-eaters that vegetarian food is not only good for you, but tasty, too.

# Tips for Successful Cooking

- Use metric or imperial measurements only; do not mix the two.

- Use measuring spoons: 1 tsp = 5ml; 1 tbsp = 15ml

- All spoon measurements are level unless otherwise stated.

- All eggs are medium unless otherwise stated.

- Recipes using raw or lightly cooked eggs should not be given to babies, pregnant woman, the very old or anyone suffering from or recovering from an illness.

- The cooking times are an approximate guide only. If you are using a fan oven reduce the cooking time according to the manufacturer's instructions.

- Ovens should be preheated to the required temperature.

- Fruits and vegetables should be washed before use.

Please note: most of the recipes have ingredients listed for a number of servings. If the recipe includes servings for two and four people, for example, the recipe will show how much to add for two people, with the amount for four people in brackets, i.e., 2 tbsp (4 tbsp).

# snacks
### and starters

# Baba Ghanoush

*Easy Entertaining*

A creamy, smoky, spiced dip that can be served with crudités or spread on toast.

### Serves 2

1 small aubergine
2 tbsp tahini
1 tbsp lemon juice
1 small clove garlic, peeled and crushed
½ tsp ground cumin
¼ tsp chilli powder
1 tbsp fresh coriander, chopped, plus extra for garnish
salt and freshly ground black pepper
1 small rustic loaf

### Serves 4

1 large aubergine
4 tbsp tahini
2 tbsp lemon juice
1 clove garlic, peeled and crushed
1 tsp ground cumin
½ tsp chilli powder
2 tbsp fresh coriander, chopped, plus extra for garnish
salt and freshly ground black pepper
1 small rustic loaf

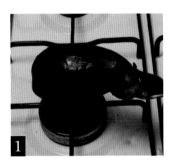

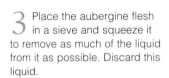

1 Using a large fork or similar implement, spear the aubergine firmly. You need to do this so that you can then slowly roast it over a gas flame until the aubergine becomes soft, tender and shrivelled and the skin is blackened. This will take a few minutes. It can be baked in the oven but it does not give the same flavour.

2 Leave the aubergine until cool enough to handle. Use your fingers to peel away all the skin and discard. You may need to rinse the aubergine quickly under the tap to remove any last scraps of charred skin.

3 Place the aubergine flesh in a sieve and squeeze it to remove as much of the liquid from it as possible. Discard this liquid.

4 Now place the aubergine in a food processor, or blender, with the tahini, lemon juice, garlic, cumin and chilli powder and process until smooth. Spoon the mixture into a bowl and stir through the chopped coriander. Season to taste.

5 Thickly slice the loaf and toast both sides. Serve the baba ghanoush spooned onto the toast, garnish with a little more coriander and serve.

# Houmous

*Children's Choice*

Always popular, houmous makes a delicious snack or party dip.

## Serves 2

1 x 200g/7oz can chick peas, drained and rinsed (or 60g/2½oz dried chick peas)
1 small pinch cayenne pepper (optional)
1 tsp olive oil
2 large flour tortillas
1 tbsp tahini
2 tbsp olive oil
1 clove garlic, peeled and crushed
juice of ½ lemon
1 tsp ground cumin
salt and freshly ground black pepper
1 small pinch cayenne pepper

## Serves 4

1 x 400g/14oz can chick peas, drained and rinsed (or 125g/5oz dried chick peas)
1 pinch cayenne pepper (optional)
2 tsp olive oil
2 large flour tortillas
3 tbsp tahini
4 tbsp olive oil
2 cloves garlic, peeled and crushed
juice of 1 lemon
2 tsp ground cumin
salt and freshly ground black pepper
1 pinch cayenne pepper

1 Soak dried chick peas overnight in plenty of cold water, then drain. Place them in a large saucepan and cover with cold water. Bring to the boil. Cook at a rolling boil for 10 minutes, removing any scum that rises to the surface.

2 Reduce the heat to a gentle simmer and cook covered for approximately 1½ hours, or until tender, drain.

3 Preheat the oven to 220°C/425°F/Gas 7. Mix the oil and the cayenne pepper together if using. Lightly brush the tortillas with the oil and cut into wedges. Place on a baking sheet and cook 8–10 minutes or until they are lightly golden and crisp. Cool on a wire rack.

4 Place all the ingredients, except the salt and pepper, in a food processor and blend until smooth. If the mixture is particularly thick you may need to add a little water. Season, and sprinkle with a pinch of cayenne pepper. Serve with pitta bread, crudités or tortilla wedges (see p.100).

# Mexican Bean Soup

One Pot

A real winter warmer, this soup is almost a meal in itself. Serve it with plenty of crusty bread, and no one will go hungry.

## Serves 2

1 tbsp oil
1 onion, peeled and finely
   chopped
1 clove garlic, peeled and
   crushed
½ red pepper, deseeded and
   finely chopped
1 tsp paprika
¼ tsp chilli powder
½ tsp ground cumin
1 tbsp tomato purée
1 x 200g/7oz can chopped
   tomatoes
½ avocado
1 x 200g/7oz can red kidney
   beans
½ tbsp vinegar
½ tsp sugar
salt and freshly ground
   black pepper
sour cream and chilli powder
   to serve (optional)

## Serves 4

2 tbsp oil
2 onions, peeled and finely
   chopped
2 cloves garlic, peeled and
   crushed
1 red pepper, deseeded and
   finely chopped
2 tsp paprika
½ tsp chilli powder
1 tsp ground cumin
2 tbsp tomato purée
1 x 400g/14oz can chopped
   tomatoes
1 avocado
1 x 400g/14oz can red kidney
   beans
1 tbsp vinegar
1 tsp sugar
salt and freshly ground
   black pepper
sour cream and chilli powder
   to serve (optional)

1 In a large saucepan heat the oil and cook the onion gently until soft. Stir in the garlic and red pepper and continue to cook until the pepper is softened.

2 Add the spices and cook, stirring, over a moderate heat for 3 minutes. Stir in the purée and tomatoes and simmer gently for 15 minutes. Remove from the heat and allow to cool a little. Either use a hand blender or food processor to liquidise the soup until it is almost smooth. Return the mixture to the pan with 150ml/¼ pt (300ml/½pt) water

3 Peel and mash the avocado and stir into the soup along with the kidney beans, vinegar and sugar. Cook for a further 15 minutes. Season to taste and serve with sour cream and a sprinkling of chilli powder if desired.

# Onion Soup with Cheese & Mustard Toasts

*One Pot*

Patience will give this soup the dark, rich colour that it normally at least partly derives from beef stock. The slow caramelisation process creates flavour and colour, making it well worth the time required.

### Serves 2

**450g/1lb onions, peeled**
**40g/1½oz butter**
**500ml/18fl oz vegetable stock**
**salt and freshly ground**
    **black pepper**
**small baguette**
**40g/1½oz cheddar cheese,**
    **grated**
**½ tbsp Dijon mustard**

### Serves 4

**900g/2lb onions, peeled**
**75g/3oz butter**
**1l/1¾pt vegetable stock**
**salt and freshly ground**
    **black pepper**
**1 small baguette**
**75g/3oz cheddar cheese,**
    **grated**
**1 tbsp Dijon mustard**

1 Slice the onions as thinly as you can. If you have a mandolin or thin slicing attachment on your food processor this is ideal. Melt the butter in a large saucepan and add the onions, stirring well to coat in the butter.

2 Now take a large piece of greaseproof paper and screw it up. Then splash it with cold water shaking off any excess. Now straighten this out and use to cover the surface of the onions, tucking it in at the edges and being careful not to burn yourself.

3 Allow the onions to cook like this for about 20 minutes, then remove the paper and discard. Continue to cook, stirring from time to time, until the onions start to turn a deep golden brown and almost caramelise in places.

4 Add the stock and bring to the boil, reduce the heat to a gentle simmer and cook for a further 10 minutes. Season to taste. Preheat the grill to high. Thickly slice the French bread, mix the grated cheese with the mustard and divide between the slices of bread. Toast until melted and golden. Serve ladled into bowls, topped with the toasted cheese and bread.

# Smoked Sweet-potato & Chilli Soup

*Easy Entertaining*

This is an easy-to-make soup that is just as good as a Saturday lunch after tearing around the supermarket as it is as a starter at a dinner party.

## Serves 2

½ tbsp oil
1 small onion, peeled and
    chopped
1 small clove garlic, peeled
    and crushed
¼ tsp dried red-chilli flakes
½ tbsp smoked paprika
250g/9oz sweet potatoes,
    peeled & cut into chunks
500ml/18fl oz vegetable stock
salt and freshly ground
    black pepper
3 tbsp crème fraîche

## Serves 4

1 tbsp oil
1 onion, peeled and chopped
1 clove garlic, peeled and
    crushed
½ tsp dried red-chilli flakes
1 tbsp smoked paprika
500g/1lb 2oz sweet potatoes,
peeled & cut into chunks
1l/1¾pt vegetable stock
salt and freshly ground
    black pepper
6 tbsp crème fraîche

1 In a large saucepan heat the oil over a moderate heat and cook the onion until it softens. Now add the garlic, chilli flakes and paprika and cook for 3 minutes, stirring well to mix.

2 Now add the sweet potatoes and toss well to coat in the spiced onion mixture. Cover with a lid, turn the heat to low and let the mixture cook for 5 minutes. Pour in the vegetable stock and increase the heat to bring up to boiling point. Stir well, then reduce the heat to

simmering and cook covered for 20 minutes.

3 Remove the pan from the heat and allow to cool a little. Then purée the mixture with a hand blender or a food processor. Be very careful as sometimes hot liquids can splash out when processed.

4 Once smooth return the mixture to the pan and bring gently back to the boil. Season to taste and stir through the crème fraîche before serving.

# Mushroom & Garlic Soup

## Children's Choice

Because this soup tastes delicious when made with mushrooms, the variety doesn't matter. If you wish, simply buy the cheapest. Mushrooms have such a meaty texture that this is a soup for the unconverted.

### Serves 2

1 tbsp oil
15g/½oz butter
1 small onion, peeled and
   chopped
2 cloves garlic, peeled and
   finely chopped
300g/10½oz assorted
   mushrooms, cleaned
   (and sliced if large)
1 tbsp plain flour
375ml/13fl oz vegetable stock
1 tbsp fresh parsley, chopped
salt and freshly ground
   black pepper
crusty bread to serve

### Serves 4

2 tbsp oil
25g/1oz butter
1 onion, peeled and chopped
4 cloves garlic, peeled and
   finely chopped
600g/1lb 5oz assorted
   mushrooms, cleaned
   (and sliced if large)
2 tbsp plain flour
750ml/1¼pt vegetable stock
2 tbsp fresh parsley,
   chopped
salt and freshly ground
   black pepper
crusty bread to serve

1 In a large saucepan heat the oil and butter over a moderate heat. Add the onion and garlic and cook gently until the onion is softened and transparent.

2 Add the mushrooms and stir well to coat in the buttery mixture. Turn the heat to low and cook covered with a well-fitting lid for 15 minutes, shaking the pan from time to time.

3 Remove the lid and sprinkle over the flour, using a wooden spoon stir to mix. Continue stirring over the heat for 2 minutes. Now add about a third of the stock, stirring well to mix.

4 Add the remaining stock, stir well and bring gently to the boil. Simmer gently for 10 minutes, then stir in the parsley. Season to taste and serve with crusty bread.

# Minestrone

## Low Cal

This is traditionally a summer soup as this is when the vegetables that go into it would have ripened in the past. Thanks to the year-round availability of its ingredients today, you can now make this soup any time that you like.

### Serves 2

2 ripe tomatoes
1½ tbsp olive oil
1 onion, peeled and finely
    chopped
1 carrot, peeled
100g/4oz potatoes, peeled
½ stick celery
1 small courgette
½ x 200g/7oz tin cannellini
    beans
450ml/¾pt vegetable stock
50g/2oz soup pasta
2 tbsp vegetarian Parmesan
    cheese, grated
salt and freshly ground
    black pepper

### Serves 4

4 ripe tomatoes
3 tbsp olive oil
1 large onion, peeled and
    finely chopped
2 carrots, peeled
225g/8oz potatoes, peeled
1 stick celery
1 courgette
1 x 200g/7oz tin cannellini
    beans
900ml/1½pt vegetable stock
100g/4oz soup pasta
4 tbsp vegetarian Parmesan
    cheese, grated
salt and freshly ground
    black pepper

1 Using a sharp knife cut a cross in the base of each tomato and place in a large mixing bowl. Cover with boiling water and leave to stand for 2 minutes, drain and peel. Chop into small chunks and set to one side.

2 Heat the olive oil in a large saucepan and cook the onions until transparent. Chop the carrot, potato, celery and courgette into small dice. Add the carrot and potato to the onions and stir well, cooking for 3–4 minutes. Add the celery and courgette, stirring to mix and cook for a further 3 minutes.

3 Stir in the cannellini beans and the prepared tomatoes. Pour over the stock and bring gently to the boil. Reduce the heat to a gentle simmer and cook for 40 minutes. Add the pasta and continue to cook for 10 minutes. Stir in the Parmesan and season to taste before serving.

# Sweet-potato Wedges with Tzatziki

*Children's Choice*

Best piping hot, these wedges will disappear before your eyes. If the potatoes become a little burnt at the edges, it doesn't matter as they just caramelise.

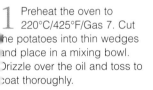

## Serves 2

450g/1lb sweet potatoes, peeled
1½ tbsp oil
½ tsp paprika
½ tsp cumin
½ tsp chilli powder
½ tsp salt
100ml/3½fl oz Greek-style yoghurt
1 small clove garlic, peeled and crushed
5cm-/2in-piece cucumber
2 tbsp fresh mint, chopped
½ tbsp olive oil
salt and freshly ground black pepper

## Serves 4

900g/2lb sweet potatoes, peeled
3 tbsp oil
1 tsp paprika
1 tsp cumin
1 tsp chilli powder
1 tsp salt
200ml/7fl oz Greek-style yoghurt
1 clove garlic, peeled and crushed
10cm-/4in-piece cucumber
4 tbsp fresh mint, chopped
1 tbsp olive oil
salt and freshly ground black pepper

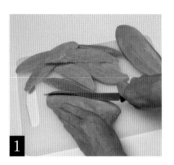

1 Preheat the oven to 220°C/425°F/Gas 7. Cut the potatoes into thin wedges and place in a mixing bowl. Drizzle over the oil and toss to coat thoroughly.

2 Mix together the paprika, cumin, chilli powder and salt. Sprinkle this mixture over the potato wedges. Line a large baking tray with non-stick parchment paper. Spread the spiced wedges in a single layer over the lined baking

tray. Cook for 25 minutes, turning once half way thorough, until golden and cooked thorough.

3 Meanwhile mix the yoghurt and garlic together in a bowl. Halve the cucumber and deseed with a teaspoon. Cut into small dice and add to the yoghurt along with the mint and oil. Mix and season to taste. Serve with the potato wedges.

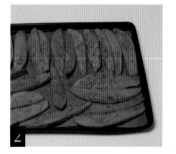

# Stuffed Mushrooms

*Easy Entertaining*

If the mushrooms are particularly large, they could be served as a main course.

## Serves 2

2 thick slices wholemeal
    bread
½ tbsp olive oil, plus extra for
    brushing over
1 small clove garlic, peeled
1 tbsp fresh parsley,
    chopped
2 large field mushrooms,
    cleaned
1 tomato, thickly sliced
2 thick slices Brie cheese
salt and freshly ground
    black pepper
basil sprigs to garnish

## Serves 4

4 thick slices wholemeal
    bread
1 tbsp olive oil, plus extra for
    brushing over
1 clove garlic, peeled
2 tbsp fresh parsley,
    chopped
4 large field mushrooms,
    cleaned
1 large tomato, thickly sliced
4 thick slices Brie cheese
salt and freshly ground
    black pepper
basil sprigs to garnish

1 Preheat the oven to 200°C/ 400°F/Gas 6. Using a sharp knife or a large pastry cutter, cut circles from the bread slices as large or slightly larger than the mushrooms. Brush lightly with a little olive oil, place on a baking sheet and set to one side.

2 Take the scraps of bread and blend in a food processor or blender to form coarse breadcrumbs; you should have about 50g/2oz (100g/4oz). If you need to, add a little extra bread to make up to the required quantity. Heat the oil in a frying pan, crush

the clove of garlic and add to the pan with the breadcrumbs. Stir until they start to turn golden and crisp, remove from the heat and add the parsley.

3 Remove the stalks from the mushrooms and discard. Brush lightly with oil and place each mushroom on a disc of bread. Top with a tomato slice and then the breadcrumb mixture, finishing each one with a slice of Brie. Bake in the preheated oven for 15–20 minutes until the mushrooms are tender. Season to taste and serve.

# Coriander & Lentil Soup

*Low cal*

Lentils are not only cheap but also full of fibre and protein.

## Serves 2

½ tbsp sunflower oil
1 onion, peeled and finely
    chopped
1 small clove garlic, peeled
    and crushed
1.25cm-/½in-piece fresh root
    ginger, peeled and finely
    grated
75g/3oz red lentils, washed
600ml/1pt vegetable stock
3 tbsp fresh coriander,
    chopped
salt and freshly ground
    black pepper
chunks of bread to serve

## Serves 4

1 tbsp sunflower oil
1 large onion, peeled and
    finely chopped
1 clove garlic, peeled and
    crushed
2.5cm-/1in-piece fresh root
    ginger, peeled and finely
    grated
175g/6oz red lentils, washed
    and drained
1.2l/2pt vegetable stock
6 tbsp fresh coriander,
    chopped
salt and freshly ground
    black pepper
chunks of bread to serve

1 Heat the oil in a large saucepan over a moderate heat and cook the onion and garlic until softened. Add the ginger and cook for 1–2 minutes stirring.

2 Stir in the washed and drained lentils mixing well to coat in the onion and oil mixture.

3 Pour over the vegetable stock and bring to the boil. Reduce the heat to a gentle simmer and cook for 30 minutes stirring from time to time.

4 Remove from the heat and stir through the chopped coriander. Season to taste. If you prefer a smoother soup you can blend it in a food processor or blender at this point. Be careful as the soup may splash out as you blend. I often cover the lid with a clean tea towel to avoid being scalded. Serve with chunks of bread.

# Thai Soup

*One Pot*

This soup mixes many flavours together – spicy, sweet and creamy.

### Serves 2

1½ shallots
50g/2oz small mushrooms
50g/2oz baby corn
1 red chilli
1.25cm-/½in-piece fresh root
    ginger
1 stalk lemon grass
½ tbsp oil
50g/2oz tofu, drained & sliced
225ml/8fl oz vegetable stock
150ml/¼pt coconut milk
50g/2oz bean sprouts
½ tsp soft brown sugar
½ small bunch coriander,
    roughly chopped
salt and freshly ground
    black pepper

### Serves 4

3 shallots
100g/4oz small mushrooms
100g/4oz baby corn
1–2 red chillies
2.5cm-/1in-piece fresh root
    ginger
2 stalks lemon grass
1 tbsp oil
100g/4oz tofu, drained & sliced
450ml/¾pt vegetable stock
300ml/½pt coconut milk
100g/4oz bean sprouts
1 tsp soft brown sugar
1 small bunch coriander,
    roughly chopped
salt and freshly ground
    black pepper

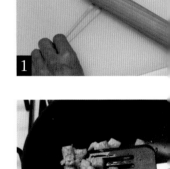

1 Peel the shallots and slice into thin wedges. Quarter any large mushrooms. Halve the baby corn. Deseed and finely slice the chilli. Peel and finely grate the ginger. Discard the tough outer layers from the lemon grass and then bruise with a rolling pin.

2 Heat the oil in a wok or large saucepan and cook the tofu over a moderate heat, turning frequently until golden. Remove with a slotted spoon and drain on kitchen paper.

3 Add the sliced shallots to the pan and cook until soft. Stir in the mushrooms and cook for 2–3 minutes. Add the baby corn, chillies and ginger and cook for 3 minutes, stirring. Add the lemon grass.

4 Pour the stock and coconut milk over the vegetables. Bring to the boil, then simmer for 5 minutes.

5 Stir in the bean sprouts and cook for 1–2 minutes until piping hot. Remove from the heat and stir in the sugar. Roughly chop the coriander and stir it through, reserving a little for garnish. Season, sprinkle with tofu and garnish.

# Mushroom & Garlic Paté

*Easy Entertaining*

The texture of this paté will depend on how finely you chop the mushrooms.

## Serves 2

15g/½oz unsalted butter
½ small onion, peeled and
    finely chopped
1 small clove garlic, peeled
    and crushed
200g/7oz button mushrooms,
    finely chopped
¼ tsp dried mixed herbs
1 tbsp dry sherry
1 tbsp cream cheese
1 tbsp fresh parsley, chopped
salt and freshly ground
    black pepper
toast to serve

## Serves 4

25g/1oz unsalted butter
1 small onion, peeled and
    finely chopped
1 clove garlic, peeled and
    crushed
400g/14oz button mushrooms,
    finely chopped
½ tsp dried mixed herbs
3 tbsp dry sherry
2 tbsp cream cheese
2 tbsp fresh parsley,
    chopped
salt and freshly ground
    black pepper
toast to serve

1 Melt the butter in a large saucepan and cook the onion and garlic over a moderate heat until softened.

2 Add the mushrooms stirring well to mix. Cook for 5 minutes until the mushrooms start to soften. Sprinkle over the mixed herbs and stir.

3 Reduce the heat to a gentle simmer and cook uncovered, stirring from time to time until the mixture is looking

dry. Stir in the sherry and continue to cook for 4–5 minutes.

4 Remove from the heat and leave to cool.

5 Beat in the cream cheese. Stir through the parsley and season to taste before serving with fresh toast.

# Cheese & Walnut Straws

*Children's Choice*

Nobody can resist freshly baked cheese straws. Although I have provided quantities for two people, restrict yourself to these, and you'll probably wish that you'd made more!

### Serves 2

**50g/2oz plain flour**
**40g/1½oz butter, chilled**
**25g/1oz mature cheddar**
**cheese**
**15g/½oz Parmesan cheese**
**1 pinch cayenne pepper**
**40g/1½oz walnut pieces**
**1 beaten egg for brushing over**
**salt and freshly ground**
**black pepper**

### Serves 4

**100g/4oz plain flour**
**75g/3oz butter, chilled**
**50g/2oz mature cheddar**
**cheese**
**25g/1oz Parmesan cheese**
**¼ tsp cayenne pepper**
**75g/3oz walnut pieces**
**1 beaten egg for brushing over**
**salt and freshly ground**
**black pepper**

1 Sift the flour into a bowl and then working quickly coarsely grate the butter into the flour. You will need to keep dipping the butter into the flour and sprinkling flour over the grater, to stop the butter from sticking but the end result is worth it.

2 Once this is done stir the mixture quickly with a knife to incorporate the butter through the flour. Place in the freezer for a few minutes to chill while you make the filling.

3 Coarsely grate the cheddar cheese into a bowl. Finely grate the

Parmesan and add it to the bowl along with the cayenne pepper. Coarsely chop the walnuts and add to the cheese mixture.

4 Preheat the oven to 220°C/425°F/Gas7. Remove the bowl from the freezer and add enough cold water to make a firm dough. It is always best to add the water a little at a time, as if you add too much water it will make the pastry tough (as does over-handling). Stir the water in with a knife, until it looks like you have almost added enough. Now use your fingertips and bring it quickly together.

**5**

**6**

5 On a lightly floured surface roll out the pastry to a thickness of 5mm/¼in using a rolling pin. Brush the surface with a thin coating of the beaten egg. Now sprinkle a third of the cheese mixture over half of the pastry. Fold the uncovered piece of pastry over the cheese and nuts, pressing down well with the rolling pin to seal.

6 Give the pastry a quarter turn. Roll out again to 5mm/¼in and repeat the whole procedure. Now brush the top of the pastry lightly with the egg and sprinkle over the remaining cheese and walnuts, pressing down to seal. Cut into thin strips and place on a baking sheet, allowing room between each one to rise. Bake in the oven for 10–12 minutes. Cool on a wire rack and serve.

# pies,
# tarts and
# quiches

# Mushroom & Ale Pie

## Easy Entertaining

I first tasted this pie in a traditional English pub. Make sure that you serve it with plenty of bread or potatoes to soak up all of that lovely, rich gravy.

### Serves 2

1 onion, peeled
300g/10½oz mushrooms
15g/½oz butter
½ tbsp oil
1 small clove garlic, peeled
    and crushed
½ stick celery, sliced
2 tbsp plain flour
150ml/¼pt brown ale
1 tsp Dijon mustard
1 tbsp fresh parsley, chopped
salt and freshly ground
    black pepper
250g/9oz puff pastry
1 beaten egg, small
crusty bread or cooked
    potatoes
a cooked vegetable of your
    choice

### Serves 4

2 onions, peeled
600g/1lb 2oz mushrooms
25g/1oz butter
1 tbsp oil
1 clove garlic, peeled and
    crushed
1 stick celery, sliced
4 tbsp plain flour
300ml/½pt brown ale
2 tsp Dijon mustard
2 tbsp fresh parsley, chopped
salt and freshly ground
    black pepper
500g/1lb 2oz puff pastry
1 beaten egg
crusty bread or cooked
    potatoes
a cooked vegetable of your
    choice

1 Using a sharp knife slice the onions into thin wedges. Thickly slice the mushrooms. If some are small leave them whole.

2 Heat oil and butter in a large pan and cook the onions and garlic over a moderate heat until they soften. Add the celery and cook for a further 2–3 minutes.

3 Add the mushrooms and stir well to coat in the onion and celery mixture. Cover and cook over a gentle heat, stirring from time to time until the mushrooms change colour and soften (about 10 minutes).

4 Sprinkle over the flour and cook, stirring, for 1 minute, until all the flour is mixed in and any juices that have collected are absorbed.

5 Add a little of the ale and stir well to mix; it will thicken quite quickly at this point. Continue adding the ale a little at a time until it is all incorporated. Simmer gently for 5 minutes. Remove from the heat. Stir in the mustard and parsley and season to taste. Pour into a 600ml/1pt (1.2l/2pt) deep pie dish. If using individual ones, divide the mixture equally between them. Set to one side to cool a little.

6 Preheat the oven to 200°C/400°F/Gas 6. Roll out the pastry on a well-floured surface to approximately 1cm/½in thick. Brush the edges of the pie dish with a little water. Cut thin strips of pastry

and press them around the edge of the pie dish. Brush this pastry edge with a little more water. Now take the larger piece of pastry and drape over the pie dish, then cut away the excess. Use the pastry scraps to decorate the top of the pie, if you wish. Brush with beaten egg to glaze. Using a sharp knife cut 2–3, 3cm/2in slashes in the middle of the pastry to allow steam to escape during cooking.

7 Bake in the preheated oven for 25–30 minutes. Serve with crusty bread or potatoes and a vegetable of your choice.

# Three-Tomato Tart

*Children's Choice*

This light tart tastes as good warm as it does cold. Serve it with a green salad and potatoes.

Serves 4-6

100g/4oz wholemeal flour
50g/2oz plain flour
1 tsp paprika
50g/4oz butter or margarine
50g/2oz rolled oats
1 x 400g/14oz can chopped tomatoes
1 tbsp tomato purée
1 tbsp balsamic vinegar
150g/5oz cherry tomatoes
2 eggs, beaten
2 tbsp single cream
50g/2oz Parmesan cheese, finely grated
salt and freshly ground black pepper
basil to garnish

1 Place the flours and paprika in a bowl and add the butter or margarine. Cut the fat into small pieces using a knife. Using your fingertips, rub the fat into the flour until the mixture resembles rough breadcrumbs. Add the oats and mix thoroughly. Stir in 3–4 tbsp of cold water stirring with a knife to mix. If you need to add a little more do so, but add it gradually or you risk making the pastry tough. Use your hands to bring the mixture together to form a dough. Place in the fridge to chill for at least 30 minutes.

2 Remove the pastry from the fridge. On a lightly floured surface roll the pastry out to a thickness of 1cm/½in and use to line a 23cm/9in tart tin. Return the pastry to the fridge to chill again for 30 minutes.

3 Preheat the oven to 190°C/375°F/Gas 5 and heat a baking sheet. Empty the can of tomatoes into a saucepan, add the tomato purée and balsamic vinegar. Cook over a moderate heat until the mixture thickens. Remove from the heat and allow to cool a little. Slice the cherry tomatoes in half and stir into the cooled tomato mixture along with the eggs, cream, cheese and salt and pepper to taste.

4 Line the chilled pastry case with greaseproof paper and fill with baking beans. Place on the preheated baking sheet and cook for 10 minutes. Remove the greaseproof paper and baking beans and cook the pastry case for a further 5 minutes.

5 Pour the tomato mixture into the pastry case and cook for 30 minutes until golden and set.

# Carrot & Rocket Rice Tart

*Easy Entertaining*

This tart has an unusual crust. The stock and thyme flavour the rice, while the baking makes it crisp around the edges.

## Serves 4-6

**25g/1oz butter**
**4 large shallots, peeled and chopped**
**2 cloves garlic, peeled and crushed**
**225g/8 oz brown rice**
**900ml/1½pt vegetable stock**
**1 tsp dried thyme**
**450g/1lb carrots, peeled and coarsely grated**
**50g/2oz rocket**
**75g/3oz mature cheddar cheese, grated**
**2 eggs**
**8 tbsp Greek yoghurt**
**salt and freshly ground black pepper**

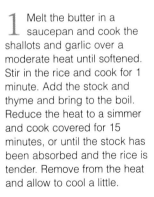

1 Melt the butter in a saucepan and cook the shallots and garlic over a moderate heat until softened. Stir in the rice and cook for 1 minute. Add the stock and thyme and bring to the boil. Reduce the heat to a simmer and cook covered for 15 minutes, or until the stock has been absorbed and the rice is tender. Remove from the heat and allow to cool a little.

2 Preheat the oven to 190°C/ 375°F/Gas 5 and preheat a heavy baking sheet. Place the carrots, rocket and cheese in a bowl and mix together. Beat one of the eggs and add, along with the yoghurt. Season to taste.

3 Beat the remaining egg into the rice mixture. Season to taste. Press the rice mixture into a 23cm/9in deep tart tin, pressing it up the sides to cover.

4 Cook the lined tart tin for 10 minutes on the preheated baking sheet. Now add the carrot mixture and return the tart to the oven for 30 minutes until golden and set.

# Creamy Courgette Tart

*Easy Entertaining*

Some supermarkets sell ready-made pastry cases, and if you are in a hurry, you could use one of these instead of the shortcrust pastry specified in the list of ingredients.

**Serves 4-6**

**400g/14oz shortcrust pastry**
**450g/1lb courgettes**
**150g/5oz soft garlic-and-herb cheese**
**1 egg**
**salt and freshly ground black pepper**

1 On a lightly floured surface roll out the pastry and use to line a 23cm/9in shallow, loose-bottomed tart tin. Trim the excess pastry with a small, sharp knife. Chill the pastry for 30 minutes. Preheat the oven to 200°C/400°F/Gas 6 and place a baking sheet in the oven to heat.

2 Line the pastry case with a piece of greaseproof paper and then fill with baking beans. Bake the pastry case on the preheated baking sheet for 10 minutes. Remove the greaseproof paper and the baking beans and return the pastry case to the oven for a further 5 minutes. Set to one side while you make the filling.

3 Wash and trim the courgettes. Coarsely grate into a bowl.

4 In a small bowl beat the cheese a little to loosen. In a small bowl beat the egg and then add a little at a time to the cheese, beating well between each addition.

5 Mix the cheese mixture into the courgettes. Season with salt and pepper. Fill the pastry case with this mixture, levelling a little with the back of a spoon.

6 Place in the oven on the baking sheet and cook for 30 minutes, or until set. Remove and allow to cool for 10 minutes before serving.

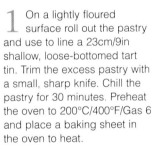
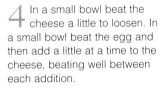
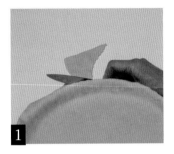

# Rustic Pie

*Easy Entertaining*

This colourful pie tastes good at any time of year. Serve it hot or at room temperature.

## Serves 4-6

100g/4oz wholemeal flour
100g/4oz plain flour
100g/4oz butter or margarine, diced
250g/9oz small new potatoes
2 tbsp olive oil
1 red onion, peeled and thinly sliced
2 red peppers, deseeded and thinly sliced
100g/4oz feta cheese, crumbled
salt and freshly ground black pepper
1 beaten egg

1 Place the flours in a bowl and add margarine or butter. Rub the fat into the flour with your fingertips until the mixture resembles rough breadcrumbs. Stir in 4 tbsp cold water with a knife. Use your hands to form the mixture into a dough. Chill for at least 30 minutes in fridge.

2 Place the potatoes in a pan of boiling water and cook for 10 minutes until tender. Drain and cut into quarters when cooled.

3 Heat the oil in a large frying pan and cook the onion and pepper over a moderate heat for 5–8 minutes, stirring from time to time until softened. Remove from the heat and stir in the potatoes. Cool.

4 Remove the pastry from the fridge. On a lightly floured surface roll the pastry out in a rough circle to a thickness of 6mm/¼in. Place on a lightly oiled baking sheet.

5 Add the feta cheese, along with salt and pepper to taste, to the potato and peppers. Pile this mixture into the middle of the pastry. Brush the edges with beaten egg. Roughly draw up the edges, pinching together to form an edge. Bake in the preheated oven for 30 minutes. Serve.

# Puff-pastry Squares with Pesto, Tomatoes & Walnuts

*Easy Entertaining*

You could either serve these squares just as they are as a starter or else team them with salad and potatoes to make more of a meal.

## Serves 2

**250g/9oz puff pastry**
**15g/½oz rocket**
**3 large basil leaves**
**1 small clove garlic, peeled and crushed**
**½ tbsp pine nuts**
**2½ tbsp Parmesan cheese, finely grated**
**1 tbsp olive oil**
**1 beaten egg**
**100g/3oz cherry tomatoes**
**25g/1oz walnut pieces**
**salt and freshly ground black pepper**

## Serves 4

**500g/1lb 2oz puff pastry**
**25g/1oz rocket**
**6 large basil leaves**
**1 clove garlic, peeled and crushed**
**1 tbsp pine nuts**
**5 tbsp Parmesan cheese, finely grated**
**2 tbsp olive oil**
**1 beaten egg**
**200g/7oz cherry tomatoes**
**50g/2oz walnut pieces**
**salt and freshly ground black pepper**

1 Roll out the pastry to 6mm/¼in thick. Cut 2 (4) 15cm/6in squares from the pastry. Use a sharp knife to mark a border around each square approximately 2.5cm/1in in from the edge. Place on a baking tray and chill until ready to use.

2 Preheat the oven to 200°C/400°F/Gas 6. Process the rocket, basil, garlic, pine nuts and half the Parmesan in a food processor or blender until roughly

chopped. Add the oil and process until smooth. Divide this mixture between the pastry pieces, spreading it up to the knife-marked border. Brush the border edge with beaten egg.

3 Quarter the tomatoes and divide between the pastry squares. Sprinkle with walnuts and remaining Parmesan. Season with salt and pepper. Brush the pastry with beaten egg and bake in the preheated oven for 15–20 minutes until golden and crisp.

# Vegetable Pasties with Horseradish & Thyme

*Children's choice*

Packed full of vegetables, these pasties are good to have to hand for lunchboxes and picnics. They may be served hot or cold.

## Makes 2

**100g/4oz wholemeal flour**
**50g/2oz plain flour**
**75g/3oz butter or margarine, diced**
**1 egg yolk**
**100g/4oz carrots, peeled**
**100g/4oz celeriac, peeled**
**75g/3oz potato, peeled**
**1 tbsp oil**
**1 small onion, peeled and finely chopped**
**½ tbsp creamed horseradish**
**½ tsp dried thyme**
**½ tbsp plain flour**
**salt and freshly ground black pepper**
**1 beaten egg for glazing**

## Makes 4

**225g/8oz wholemeal flour**
**100g/4oz plain flour**
**175g/6oz butter or margarine, diced**
**1 egg yolk**
**250g/9oz carrots, peeled**
**250g/9oz celeriac, peeled**
**150g/5oz potato, peeled**
**2 tbsp oil**
**1 onion, peeled and finely chopped**
**1 tbsp creamed horseradish**
**1 tsp dried thyme**
**1 tbsp plain flour**
**salt and freshly ground black pepper**
**1 beaten egg for glazing**

1 In a bowl mix the flours together and add the butter or margarine. Rub in, using your fingertips, until the mixture resembles coarse breadcrumbs. Beat the egg yolk with 2 tbsp of cold water and stir in. If you need to, add enough cold water to form a dough. Use your hands draw the mixture together to form a ball, knead briefly, then place in the fridge to chill for 30 minutes.

2 Preheat the oven to 190°C/ 375°F/Gas 5. Coarsely grate the carrots, celeriac and potato. Heat the oil in a large frying pan and cook the onion until it starts to turn golden in places. Add the grated vegetables and cook for 5 minutes, stirring well to mix. Stir in the horseradish and thyme. Sprinkle over the flour and cook for 1 minute, stirring. Season to taste and remove from the heat. Set to one side to cool.

3 On a lightly floured surface roll the pastry out and cut 2 (4) 18cm/7in circles. Divide the vegetable mixture between the pastry discs. Brush the edges of the pastry with a little egg and draw up both sides to cover the filling, pinching the pastry together to seal.

4 Place each pasty on a lightly greased baking sheet and brush with a little more egg. Bake in the oven for 25 minutes, or until golden and crisp.

# Curried Mixed-vegetable Tarts with a Poached Egg

*Easy Entertaining*

The poached egg is optional, so the choice is yours!

## Serves 2

125g/4oz shortcrust pastry
½ tbsp oil
15g/½oz butter
1 shallot, peeled and
    chopped
1 tsp curry powder
75g/3oz carrots, peeled
    and diced
75g/3oz parsnips, peeled
    and diced
75g/3oz butternut squash,
    peeled, deseeded and
    diced
50g/2oz courgettes, trimmed
    and diced
1 tbsp fresh coriander,
    chopped
salt and freshly ground
    black pepper
2 eggs

## Serves 4

250g/9oz shortcrust pastry
1 tbsp oil
25g/1oz butter
2 shallots, peeled and
    chopped
2 tsp curry powder
150g/5oz carrots, peeled
    and diced
150g/5oz parsnips, peeled
    and diced
150g/5oz butternut squash,
    peeled, deseeded and
    diced
100g/4oz courgettes,
    trimmed and diced
2 tbsp fresh coriander,
    chopped
salt and freshly ground
    black pepper
4 eggs

1 On a lightly floured
    surface roll out the pastry
and use to line 2 (4) 10cm/4in
individual deep tart tins. Chill
while you make the filling

2 Preheat the oven to
    200°C/400°F/Gas 6 and
place a baking sheet in the
oven to heat. In a large frying
pan heat the oil and butter and
cook the shallots until they
soften. Add the curry powder
and cook, stirring, over a
moderate heat for 2 minutes.

3 Add the carrots, parsnips and butternut squash, stirring well to mix. Cook them for 5 minutes, or until they start to soften and turn golden in places.

4 Add the courgette and cook for a further 3–4 minutes. Remove from the heat and stir in the coriander. Season to taste. Divide the mixture between the pastry cases. Place on the preheated baking sheet and cook for 20 minutes.

5 Bring a pan of water to the boil. Crack 1 egg at a time into a cup and then carefully add the egg to the boiling water. Cook for 2 minutes. Use a slotted spoon to remove the eggs and drain thoroughly. Top each tart with a hot poached egg, season lightly and serve.

# Root-vegetable Pie with a Creamy Mustard Sauce

*Family Favourite*

Flaky puff pastry with a rich, creamy sauce makes this pie a real winter warmer.

### Serves 2

15g/½oz butter
½ tbsp oil
1 onion, peeled and sliced
   into wedges
225g/8oz carrots, peeled and
   cut into chunks
225g/8oz swede, peeled and
   cut into chunks
1 small turnip, peeled and
   cut into chunks
1 tbsp flour
150ml/¼pt vegetable stock
150ml/¼pt single cream
1 tbsp wholegrain mustard
salt and freshly ground
   black pepper
250g/9oz puff pastry
1 beaten egg for brushing

### Serves 4

25g/1oz butter
1 tbsp oil
1 large onion, peeled and
   sliced into wedges
450g/1lb carrots, peeled and
   cut into chunks
450g/1lb swede, peeled and
   cut into chunks
1 turnip, peeled and cut into
   chunks
2 tbsp flour
300ml/½pt vegetable stock
300ml/½pt single cream
2 tbsp wholegrain mustard
salt and freshly ground
   black pepper
500g/1lb 2oz puff pastry
1 beaten egg for brushing

1 Preheat the oven to 200°C/400°F/Gas 6. In a large saucepan heat the butter and oil together over a moderate heat. Add the onion and cook until it is softened, stirring from time to time.

2 Add the carrots and swede, stirring well to mix. Cover and cook for 5 minutes. Now stir in the turnip and cook for a further 10 minutes, covered. Shake the pan from time to time to mix.

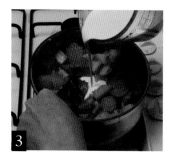

3 Sprinkle over the flour. Stirring, cook for 2 minutes, or until all the flour has been absorbed. Stir in the stock a little at a time until it has all been incorporated. Do the same with the cream. Bring gently to the boil. Remove from the heat. Stir in the mustard and season to taste.

4 Divide the mixture between 2 (4) individual ovenproof dishes. On a lightly floured surface roll out the pastry. Cut 2 (4)circles of pastry large enough to cover each dish. Brush the edge of each dish with a little water and then top with the pastry, pressing firmly round the edges to seal. Cut a steam hole in the top of each pie and brush lightly with beaten egg.

5 Bake in the preheated oven for 25 minutes or until the top is golden and crisp.

# Rich Stilton & Pear Tart

*Easy Entertaining*

Stilton and pears make a delicious combination. This tart can be served hot or at room temperature. Take it on a picnic or serve it at a buffet. It tastes particularly wonderful when teamed with a crisp, green salad.

## Serves 6-8

**50g/2oz walnuts**
**100g/4oz wholemeal flour**
**100g/4oz plain flour**
**100g/4oz butter or margarine**
**2 egg yolks**
**3 ripe dessert pears**
**150ml/¼pt milk**
**150ml/¼pt single cream**
**2 tbsp cream sherry**
**2 eggs**
**salt and freshly ground black pepper**
**50g/2oz Stilton cheese, crumbled**

1 Place the walnuts in a food processor or blender and chop coarsely. In a bowl mix the flours together. Add the butter or margarine and rub in, using your fingertips, until the mixture resembles coarse breadcrumbs. Mix in the chopped walnuts. Beat one of the egg yolks and add to the mixture along with enough cold water to form a dough. Add the water a little at a time to ensure that you don't make the mixture too wet. Use your hands to draw the mixture together to form a ball of dough. Knead briefly and place in the fridge to chill for 30 minutes.

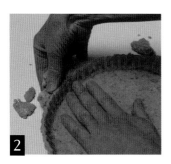

2 Preheat the oven to 190°C/ 375°F/Gas 5 and place a heavy baking sheet in the oven to heat. Roll out the pastry on a lightly floured surface and use to line a 23cm/9in loose-bottom tart tin. Return to the fridge for 20 minutes. Cover with greaseproof paper and fill with baking beans. Bake for 15 minutes on the preheated baking sheet. Remove the paper and beans and return the pastry to the oven for 5 minutes more.

3 Reduce the oven temperature to 150°C/ 300°F/Gas 2. Peel and core the pears,slice thinly and arrange over the base of the pastry case. Beat the milk, cream, sherry, eggs and remaining yolk together, seasoning with a little salt and freshly ground black pepper. Pour over the pears and then sprinkle over the Stilton. Bake on the baking sheet for 40 minutes until set. Serve hot or warm.

# Leek & Potato Pie

*Children's Choice*

Because it is open-topped, maybe this pie should be called a tart, but I tend to think of tarts as being rather delicate, and of pies as being somewhat substantial. So this is a lovely, big, chunky tart of a pie!

## Serves 4-6

**175g/6oz wholemeal flour**
**50g/2oz rolled oats**
**50g/2oz sesame seeds**
**50g/2oz mixed nuts, chopped**
**150g/5oz butter, diced**
**100g/4oz mature Cheddar cheese, coarsely grated**
**1 tbsp oil**
**250g/9oz new potatoes, boiled and cut into chunks**
**2 large leeks, washed and sliced**
**300ml/½pt milk**
**salt and freshly ground black pepper**
**1 egg yolk**

1 Preheat the oven to 200°C/ 400°F/Gas 6 and place a baking sheet in the oven to heat. Place 150g/5oz of the flour, oats, sesame seeds and nuts in bowl. Mix together and then rub in 100g/4oz of the butter. Stir through 50g/2oz of the cheese, then press this mixture into a 23cm/9in deep loose-bottomed tart tin. Bake in the preheated oven for 15-20 minutes until golden and crisp.

2 Heat the oil in a frying pan and fry the potatoes until they start to turn golden in places. Remove, using a slotted spoon, and set aside.

3 Add the remaining butter to the same pan and cook the leeks for 5 minutes or until they become tender. Sprinkle over the flour. Stir in and cook for 1 minute. Add the milk a little at a time, stirring well between each addition. Remove from the heat and season to taste. Beat in the egg yolk.

4 Pour this mixture into the prepared tin, scatter the potatoes over the surface pressing them in to level. Sprinkle over the remaining cheese and bake in the oven for 15 minutes or until the cheese is melted and golden.

# Roasted-vegetable & Mozzarella Tarts

*Easy Entertaining*

Be assured that the technique for making these puff-pastry cases is easier than it sounds! Serve these tarts with a green salad or steamed vegetables.

### Serves 2

½ red onion, peeled and cut
  into wedges
½ red pepper, deseeded and
  cut into thin strips
½ orange pepper, deseeded
  and cut into thin strips
1 tbsp olive oil
250g/9oz puff pastry
1 beaten egg
60g/2½oz mini-mozzarella balls
6 cherry tomatoes, halved
salt and freshly ground
  black pepper

### Serves 4

1 red onion, peeled and cut
  into wedges
1 red pepper, deseeded and
  cut into thin strips
1 orange pepper, deseeded
  and cut into thin strips
2 tbsp olive oil
500g/1lb 2oz puff pastry
1 beaten egg
150g/5oz mini-mozzarella balls
12 cherry tomatoes, halved
salt and freshly ground
  black pepper

1 Preheat the oven to 200°C/400°F/Gas 6. Place the onion and peppers in a roasting tin and toss together with the oil. Roast in the preheated oven for 25 minutes.

2 On a lightly floured surface roll out the pastry until it is big enough to cut out 2 (4) 15cm/6in squares. Take one square of pastry and, using a small sharp knife, cut along two edges about 2.5cm/1in in. Repeat on the other side but do not join the cuts. Now lift one corner over to the opposite inner edge.

Repeat with the other corner, so creating a raised edge. Place on a lightly greased baking tray. Repeat with the remaining pastry squares. Brush lightly with beaten egg.

3 Divide the roasted onion, peppers, mozzarella balls and cherry tomatoes between the pastry squares. Season with a little salt and freshly ground black pepper.

4 Bake in the oven for 20–25 minutes until the pastry is golden and crisp and the filling is piping hot.

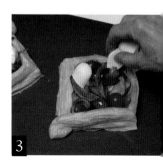

# Deep Vegetable Pie

*Easy Entertaining*

As its name suggests, this pie is both deep and packed full of roasted vegetables. If any is left over after its first serving, this could be eaten cold, or else loosely wrapped in foil before being reheated in a moderately hot oven for 20–25 minutes.

## Serves 4-6

**225g/8oz wholemeal flour**
**100g/4oz plain flour**
**200g/7oz butter or margarine, chilled**
**1 tbsp, plus 1 tsp, yeast extract, such as Marmite**
**1 egg yolk**
**250g/9oz carrots, peeled and cut into batons**
**350g/12oz baby new potatoes, halved**
**250g/9oz sweet potatoes, peeled and cut into small chunks**
**4 tbsp olive oil**
**3 large, red peppers, deseeded and cut into thin strips**
**4 sticks celery**
**2 large, red onions**
**150g/5oz button mushrooms, halved if large**
**salt and freshly ground black pepper**
**1 beaten egg**
**2 tsp dried thyme**

1 Preheat the oven to 200°C/400°F/Gas 6, and place a heavy baking sheet in the oven to heat. Sift the flour into a large mixing bowl. Toss the butter in the flour and, working quickly, cut it into small dice, stirring as you go to coat the butter in the flour. Now rub the butter into the flour until the mixture resembles breadcrumbs.

2 Dissolve the tsp of Marmite in 1 tbsp of water and beat into the egg yolk. Add this to the flour mixture, along with enough cold water to bring the mixture together to form a dough. Knead briefly and place in the fridge to chill while you make the filling.

3 Place the prepared carrots new potatoes and sweet potatoes in a large shallow roasting tin with the oil and toss to coat. Place in the preheated oven for 15 minutes.

**6**

**7**

4 Add the peppers, celery, red onions and mushrooms, stirring well to mix and coat in the oil. Return to the oven and cook for 20 minutes.

5 Remove from the oven, stir in the yeast extract, season lightly and set to one side.

6 On a lightly floured surface roll out the pastry and use to line a deep 18cm/7in tin, reserving enough

to form a lid. Pile in the roasted vegetable mixture. Brush the edges of the pastry with a little beaten egg and top with the pastry lid. Pinch round the edges to seal.

7 Cut a hole in the centre of the pastry and brush the top with the beaten egg. Place on the preheated baking tray in the oven and cook for 40 minutes until golden and crisp. Allow to stand for 10 minutes before carefully turning out. Serve cut into wedges.

grills
and fries

# Corn Fritters

*Quick and Easy*

Children love these crisp, golden fritters. Serve them piping hot with a vegetable or salad of your choice. They also taste good when teamed with a chilli dipping sauce.

## Serves 2

½ egg, beaten
½ tbsp Thai green-curry paste
125g/5oz sweet corn, canned
   or frozen
3 spring onions
½ tbsp mint
2 tbsp coriander
25g/1oz plain flour
salt and freshly ground
   black pepper
oil for shallow-frying
lime wedges & salad to serve

## Serves 4

1 egg, beaten
1 tbsp Thai green-curry paste
250g/9oz sweet corn, canned
   or frozen
6 spring onions
1 tbsp mint
4 tbsp coriander
50g/2oz plain flour
salt and freshly ground
   black pepper
oil for shallow-frying
lime wedges & salad to serve

1 In a large mixing bowl beat the egg together with the curry paste. Stir in the sweetcorn kernels.

2 Trim and finely slice the spring onions and add to the beaten egg. Remove the coarse stems from the mint and discard. Finely chop the coriander and mint.

3 Stir the chopped herbs through the sweetcorn mixture. Sprinkle over the flour and mix. Season lightly with salt and freshly ground black pepper.

4 Heat the oil in a frying pan over a moderately high heat. Cook spoonfuls of the mixture until golden, then turn and cook the other side.

5 Drain on kitchen paper and keep warm while you cook the remaining mixture.

6 Serve with lime wedges and salad.

# Sausages with Onion Gravy

*Children's Choice*

Although I recommend serving these sausages hot with mashed potatoes, if they are given the opportunity to become cold, they'll taste just as delicious!

## Serves 2

14g/½oz butter
1 red onion, peeled and
    sliced
1 vegetable stock cube
1 tsp balsamic vinegar
salt and freshly ground
    black pepper
60g/2½oz long-grain rice
½ small onion, peeled and
    very finely chopped
½ tbsp oil, plus extra for
    shallow-frying
25g/1oz wholemeal
    breadcrumbs
40g/1½oz mature Cheddar
    cheese
2 tbsp flat-leaf parsley,
    chopped
flour for coating

## Serves 4

25g/1oz butter
2 red onions, peeled and
    sliced
2 vegetable stock cubes
2 tsp balsamic vinegar
salt and freshly ground
    black pepper
150g/5oz long-grain rice
1 small onion, peeled and
    very finely chopped
1 tbsp oil, plus 2 extra for
    shallow-frying
50g/2oz wholemeal
    breadcrumbs
75g/3oz mature Cheddar
    cheese
2 tbsp flat-leaf parsley,
    chopped
flour for coating

1 In a saucepan melt the butter over a moderate heat and add the red onions, stirring well to coat in the buttery juices. Cook gently for 20 minutes, stirring from time to time until the onions start to caramelise.

2 Dissolve half of the stock cubes in 150ml/¼pt

(300ml/½pt) boiling water. Add the stock to the onions and simmer gently for 10 minutes. Stir in the balsamic vinegar and season to taste. Remove from the heat and allow to cool a little. Process in a blender or food processor until smooth. Return to the pan and keep to one side until ready to serve

3 Place the rice in a saucepan with a well fitting lid. Dissolve the stock cube in 300ml/½pt (600ml/1pt) boiling water. Pour this over the rice and bring the mixture to the boil. Now reduce the heat to a gentle simmer. Cook covered until all the liquid has been absorbed and the rice is tender. If all the liquid has not been absorbed, drain the surplus off and discard. Remove from the heat and allow to cool for 10 minutes or until cool enough to handle.

4 In a small frying pan cook the onion in the oil until it becomes softened. Remove from the heat and place in a large mixing bowl with the breadcrumbs, cheese and parsley. Add the cooled rice and mix well. Season to taste.

5 Divide the mixture into 4 (8) and shape into sausages. Roll in the flour to coat. Heat oil in a frying pan and cook the sausages over a moderate heat, turning frequently until golden on all sides and piping hot. While the sausages are cooking, place the gravy over a gentle heat and cook until piping hot. Serve with mashed potatoes

# Bean Burgers

*Children's Choice*

There are many recipes for bean burgers, but here is the one that I like to cook. If you prefer to use only one variety of beans, then do so. Serve the bean burgers with a light salad or even sandwiched in a bun with chips.

## Serves 2

½ tbsp oil
½ small onion, peeled and finely chopped
1 small clove garlic, peeled and crushed
½ tsp chilli powder
½ tsp ground cumin
1 x 200g/7oz can red kidney beans
1 x 200g/7oz can cannellini beans
½ tbsp tomato purée
2 tbsp plain flour
25g/1oz fresh brown breadcrumbs
salt and freshly ground black pepper
1 egg, beaten
dried breadcrumbs for coating
oil for frying

## Serves 4

1 tbsp oil
1 small onion, peeled and finely chopped
1 clove garlic, peeled and crushed
1 tsp chilli powder
1 tsp ground cumin
1 x 400g/14oz can red kidney beans
1 x 400g/14oz can cannellini beans
1 tbsp tomato purée
4 tbsp plain flour
50g/2oz fresh brown breadcrumbs
salt and freshly ground black pepper to taste
2 eggs, beaten
dried breadcrumbs for coating
oil for frying

1 Heat the oil in a small frying pan and cook the onions and garlic over a moderate heat until they become softened. Add the chilli powder and cumin and cook for a further minute, stirring.

2 Drain the beans and rinse well under cold running water. Leave to stand and drain for 5 minutes. Remove ¾ of the beans and mash well until almost smooth. This can be done quite easily with a potato masher. Using a fork, very roughly break up the remaining beans and then add to the smooth beans.

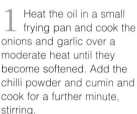

3 Stir in the tomato purée, and sautéed onion mixture, stirring well to mix. Sprinkle over the flour and breadcrumbs and season lightly with salt and pepper. Stir. Mix in enough beaten egg to make a firm mixture. Using damp hands divide the mixture into 2 (4) and shape into large patties. Chill in the fridge for 30 minutes minimum.

4 Place the remaining beaten egg in a shallow dish and the breadcrumbs in another. Dip the chilled burgers first in the beaten egg and then in the breadcrumbs, turning to coat.

5 Heat about 1cm/½in of oil in a frying pan over a moderately high heat. Once the oil is hot, carefully place the burgers in the oil and cook for 3–4 minutes on each side until golden and crisp. Remove from the pan using a fish slice. Drain on kitchen paper and serve with a light salad, or even in a bun with chips.

# Mozzarella & Veggie Fritters

*Children's Choice*

Meltingly creamy mozzarella wrapped up in carrot and courgette and then deep-fried. Delicious! Serve these fritters with a salad.

### Serves 2

**60g/2½oz mozzarella cheese**
**1 small onion**
**½ tsp salt**
**1 courgette**
**1 carrot**
**50g/2oz gram flour**
**½ tsp paprika**
**oil for deep-frying**

### Serves 4

**150g/5oz mozzarella cheese**
**1 onion**
**1 tsp salt**
**1 large courgette**
**1 large carrot**
**100g/4oz gram flour**
**1 tsp paprika**
**oil for deep-frying**

1 Drain the mozzarella, divide into 4 (8) pieces and set to one side on kitchen paper. Peel the onion and slice very thinly. This is best done on a mandolin, but if you don't have one use a very sharp knife. Lay the onion slices in a single layer on a large plate and sprinkle over the salt. Toss a little to mix. Set to one side for 15 minutes.

2 Place the onions in a plastic sieve, preferably, and rinse well under cold running water. Drain thoroughly and pat dry with kitchen paper. Coarsley grate the courgette

and carrot into a large mixing bowl. Add the dried onions and stir well to mix.

3 Sprinkle over the flour and paprika and stir. Heat the oil in a deep fat fryer. Divide the mixture into 4 (8) equal portions. Take one portion and press a piece of the drained mozzarella into the centre of it. Squeeze the mixture around the cheese to enclose it. Repeat with the remaining mixture and cheese. Now deep-fry the fritters for 4–5 minutes until they are golden and crisp. Drain on kitchen paper. Serve with salad.

# Mozzarella & Peppers in a Crusty Roll

*Quick and Easy*

The combination of crusty bread with creamy mozzarella and roasted peppers makes a perfect lunch or supper. Serve this dish as it is or with a light salad. Note that the peppers could be prepared in advance to the end of step 2 and then reheated when you are ready to eat.

## Serves 2

3 large, sweet peppers
1 tbsp olive oil
½ clove garlic, peeled and
    crushed
½ tsp paprika
60g/2½oz mozzarella cheese
2 large, crusty rolls
basil leaves to garnish
salt and freshly ground
    black pepper

## Serves 4

6 large, sweet peppers
2 tbsp olive oil
1 clove garlic, peeled and
    crushed
1 tsp paprika
150g/5oz mozzarella cheese
4 large, crusty rolls
basil leaves to garnish
salt and freshly ground
    black pepper

1 Preheat the oven to 200°C/400°F/Gas 6. Cut the peppers in half, deseed and slice into thin strips. Heat the oil in a frying pan and cook the pepper strips over a moderate heat until softened and slightly charred in places.

2 Add the garlic and sprinkle over the paprika, stirring well to mix. Continue to cook over a gentle heat for a further 5 minutes.

3 Drain the mozzarella and pat dry with kitchen paper. Slice thinly and set to one side.

4 Split the rolls in half and divide the peppers between them. Top with slices of mozzarella and cook in the preheated oven for 10 minutes, or until the cheese is melted and golden in places. Garnish with basil leaves and season to taste. Serve.

# Aubergine & Tomato Melt

## Children's Choice

Toasted sandwiches are always popular – not least with children – and this one is no exception.

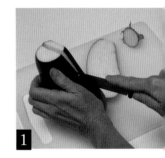

### Serves 2

1 small aubergine
2 tbsp olive oil
1 clove garlic, peeled and
   one end trimmed
2 large tomatoes, sliced
100g/4oz mature Cheddar
   cheese
4 slices crusty, wholemeal
   bread
salt and freshly ground
   black pepper

### Serves 4

1 large aubergine
4 tbsp olive oil
1 clove garlic, peeled and
   one end trimmed
4 large tomatoes, sliced
225g/8oz mature Cheddar
   cheese
8 slices crusty, wholemeal
   bread
salt and freshly ground
   black pepper

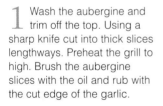

1 Wash the aubergine and trim off the top. Using a sharp knife cut into thick slices lengthways. Preheat the grill to high. Brush the aubergine slices with the oil and rub with the cut edge of the garlic.

2 Cook the aubergine slices under the preheated grill for 6–8 minutes, turning halfway through, until tender. Now top the aubergine with the sliced tomato and continue to cook for a further 5 minutes until the tomato starts to soften.

3 Preheat a griddle pan over a moderately high heat. Using a fish slice remove the aubergine and tomatoes slices and top 2 (4) of the slices of bread with them.

4 Sprinkle over the cheese and then top with the remaining slices of bread. Press down firmly and transfer to the griddle pan. Cook for 4 minutes each side until the cheese melts and the bread gets golden chargrill marks on it. Season and serve.

# Fried Halloumi with Salsa

*Children's Choice*

Slices of Greek cheese are dusted with seasoned flour and fried before being served with a fresh-tomato salsa. I would serve this dish as a light lunch or a summer supper, accompanied by crusty bread and a salad.

## Serves 2

1 large, ripe tomato
½ green chilli
2 tbsp fresh coriander
¼ tsp sugar
½ tbsp lime juice
125g/4½oz Halloumi cheese
¼ tsp chilli powder
½ tsp ground cumin
2 tbsp flour
1 tbsp oil

## Serves 4

2 large, ripe tomatoes
1 green chilli
4 tbsp fresh coriander
½ tsp sugar
1 tbsp lime juice
250g/9oz Halloumi cheese
½ tsp chilli powder
1 tsp ground cumin
4 tbsp flour
2 tbsp oil

1 Use a sharp knife to finely chop the tomatoes and place in a plastic or glass bowl. Finely chop the chilli, removing the seeds and membrane. Add the chilli to the tomatoes. Finely chop the coriander and add to the tomatoes along with the sugar and lime juice. Stir well. Set aside for at least 30 minutes to allow the flavours to develop.

2 When you are ready to eat, thinly slice the halloumi with a sharp knife. On a plate sift chilli powder and cumin together with the flour. Dip the cheese slices in the seasoned flour, turning to coat thoroughly.

3 Heat the oil in a frying pan over a moderately high heat. Cook the cheese slices for 2–3 minutes on each side until golden. Remove, using a fish slice, and drain briefly on kitchen paper. Serve with the salsa.

# Tortillas with Refried Beans

*Quick and Easy*

This Mexican flat-bread sandwich is loved by children, as well as by adults.

## Serves 2

½ tbsp olive oil, plus a little
   extra for frying
1 small onion, peeled and
   finely chopped
1 small clove garlic, peeled
   and crushed
½ green chilli, finely chopped
½ tsp paprika
½ tsp ground cumin
1 x 200g/7oz can chopped
   tomatoes
1 tbsp tomato purée
1 x 200g/7oz can red kidney
   beans, rinsed and drained
salt and freshly ground
   black pepper
4 large flour tortillas
50g/2oz feta cheese,
   crumbled
50g/2oz mature Cheddar
   cheese, grated
sour cream

## Serves 4

1 tbsp olive oil, plus a little
   extra for frying
1 onion, peeled and finely
   chopped
1 clove garlic, peeled and
   crushed
1 green chilli, finely chopped
1 tsp paprika
1 tsp ground cumin
1 x 400g/14oz can chopped
   tomatoes
2 tbsp tomato purée
1 x 400g/14oz can red kidney
   beans, rinsed and drained
salt and freshly ground
   black pepper
8 large flour tortillas
100g/4oz feta cheese,
   crumbled
100g/4oz mature Cheddar
   cheese, grated
sour cream

1 Heat the oil in a frying pan and cook the onion and garlic until soft. Add the chilli, paprika and cumin. Continue to cook, stirring, for 1 minute.

2 Add the tomatoes, tomato purée and kidney beans, stirring well to mix. Cook until the mixture becomes thick. Season to taste and remove from the heat. Using a fork, roughly mash the beans into the mixture.

3 Divide the mixture between half of the tortillas, spreading it almost to the edges. Sprinkle with the cheeses and top with the remaining tortillas.

4 Lightly oil a large frying pan and cook each tortilla over a moderate heat for about 8 minutes, turning halfway through, or until golden on each side. Serve cut into wedges with sour cream.

# Wild-mushroom & Cheese-soufflé Omelette

*Easy Entertaining*

This omelette will look rather impressive as it comes out of the pan beautifully risen and fluffed up. If you are feeding four, I suggest that you make two omelettes and divide them up. Serve the omelette with a salad or vegetables of your choice.

## Serves 2

25g/1oz butter
1 clove garlic, peeled and
    finely chopped
50g/2oz small wild
    mushrooms
4 eggs
salt and freshly ground
    black pepper
25g/1oz Parmesan cheese,
    finely grated

## Serves 4

50g/2oz butter
2 cloves garlic, peeled and
    finely chopped
100g/4oz small wild
    mushrooms
8 eggs
salt and freshly ground
    black pepper
100g/2oz Parmesan cheese,
    finely grated

1 Heat half the butter gently in a frying pan and cook the garlic for 2–3 minutes. Add the mushrooms and cook, stirring, until they soften and change colour. Remove from the pan with a slotted spoon and keep warm.

2 Separate the eggs and beat the yolks together with a little salt and pepper. Use a whisk to whip the egg whites until they reach soft peak stage. Using a large metal spoon gently fold the egg whites into the egg yolks. Preheat the grill to high.

3 In a frying pan melt the remaining butter and add the egg mixture. Cook for 2–3 minutes or until risen and golden underneath. Scatter over the mushrooms and Parmesan and place the pan under the preheated grill. Cook for 1 minute until golden in places and springy to the touch. Remove from the heat and serve with salad or vegetables of your choice.

# Welsh Rarebit

*Children's Choice*

This dish is an old favourite that should not be forgotten. Many recipes specify the inclusion of Worcestershire sauce, but even though there is now a vegetarian version of this sauce (see page 19), I have chosen not to include it.

*Serves 2*

**14g/½oz butter**
**2 spring onions, trimmed**
**    and finely sliced**
**1 pinch cayenne pepper**
**1 tsp plain flour**
**2 tbsp milk**
**75g/3oz mature Cheddar**
**    cheese, coarsely grated**
**2 thick slices bread**
**2 tsp Dijon mustard**
**salt and freshly ground**
**    black pepper**

*Serves 4*

**25g/1oz butter**
**4 spring onions, trimmed**
**    and finely sliced**
**1 pinch cayenne pepper**
**2 tsp plain flour**
**4 tbsp milk**
**175g/6oz mature Cheddar**
**    cheese, coarsely grated**
**4 thick slices bread**
**4 tsp Dijon mustard**
**salt and freshly ground**
**    black pepper**

1 In a saucepan melt the butter and cook the onions over a moderate heat for 2 minutes. Stir in the cayenne pepper and flour and cook, stirring, for 1 minute.

2 Add the milk and stir to combine, it will thicken quite quickly, so keep stirring to ensure the mixture does not become lumpy. Sprinkle over the cheese. Reduce the heat and cook gently until the cheese has melted.

3 Toast the bread on one side under a hot grill, until golden. Beat the mustard into the cheese mixture and season to taste. Divide the cheese mixture between the slices of toasted bread, spreading over the untoasted surface with a knife. Place under the grill for 1–2 minutes until the top of the cheese bubbles and turns golden in places. Serve.

# Hot Garlic-mushroom Sandwich

*Quick and Easy*

You'll probably need a napkin when you tuck into this sandwich! Thankfully, French bread is perfect for soaking up all of the buttery, garlicky juices oozing out of it.

## Serves 2

**enough crusty French bread for 2**
**4 large field mushrooms**
**50g/2oz butter**
**1 clove garlic, peeled and chopped**
**2 tbsp fresh parsley, chopped**
**salt and freshly ground black pepper**
**1 tbsp Dijon mustard**
**rocket and tomatoes to serve**

## Serves 4

**enough crusty French bread for 4**
**8 large field mushrooms**
**100g/4oz butter**
**2 cloves garlic, peeled and chopped**
**4 tbsp fresh parsley, chopped**
**salt and freshly ground black pepper**
**2 tbsp Dijon mustard**
**rocket and tomatoes to serve**

1 Preheat the oven to 190°C/375°F/Gas 5. When warm, heat the French bread for 5 minutes. Clean the mushrooms by wiping them with a damp cloth. Cut them into thick slices.

2 Melt the butter in a large frying pan and cook the garlic for 1 minute. Now add the mushrooms and cook them over a gentle heat until they have become soft and juicy.

3 Stir in the parsley and season with salt and pepper.

4 Split the warmed bread and spread it with Dijon mustard. Divide the mushrooms between the bread, pouring over the buttery juices as you do so.

5 Top with the remaining bread and serve with rocket and tomatoes.

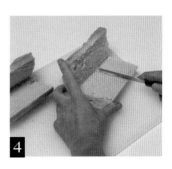

# Latkes with Eggs & Vine Tomatoes

*Children's Choice*

These potato cakes are a Jewish specialty. They are easy to prepare and go with lots of different dishes. They can easily be reheated in a hot oven for about 10 minutes until they are piping hot.

## Serves 2

**10g/4oz cherry vine tomatoes**
**1 tsp olive oil**
**1 tsp balsamic vinegar**
**salt and freshly ground**
**    black pepper**
**1 small onion, peeled**
**450g/1lb potatoes, peeled**
**25g/1oz plain flour**
**3 eggs**
**oil for shallow-frying**

## Serves 4

**225g/8oz cherry vine tomatoes**
**2 tsp olive oil**
**2 tsp balsamic vinegar**
**salt and freshly ground**
**    black pepper**
**1 onion, peeled**
**900g/2lb potatoes, peeled**
**50g/2oz plain flour**
**6 eggs**
**oil for shallow-frying**

1 Preheat the oven to 220°C/425°F/Gas 7. Place the tomatoes in a small roasting tin, toss them with the oil and vinegar, season and set to one side.

2 Finely grate the onion into a mixing bowl. Coarsely grate the potatoes and add them to the onion. Sprinkle the flour over the potato mixture. Beat one of the eggs and add it to the potato mixture, mixing well. Season with salt and pepper. Place the tomatoes in the preheated oven and cook for 10 minutes, or until the tomatoes are hot and are just starting to lose their shape.

3 Heat about 1cm/½in of oil in a frying pan over a moderate heat. Add heaped tablespoons of the potato mixture and flatten slightly. Cook for about 8 minutes, or until the latkes are golden and crisp in places, turning halfway through. Remove the latkes with a fish slice and drain them on kitchen paper. Keep them warm while you cook the eggs.

4 Crack the eggs into the hot oil and cook over a moderate heat until the white is set, or it is cooked to your preference. Top the latkes with egg and serve with the tomatoes on the side.

# Cheese & Chilli Rösti

*One Pot*

I recommend using waxy potatoes for this dish because they give the right sort of texture. Serve the rösti with a vegetable or salad of your choice. If there is any left, it can be reheated in a hot oven.

### Serves 4

**700g/1½lb waxy potatoes, peeled**
**1 onion, peeled**
**1 tbsp sunflower oil**
**15g/½oz butter**
**salt and freshly ground black pepper**
**100g/4oz cheddar cheese**
**1 tsp chilli powder**
**3 tbsp fresh parsley, chopped**

1 Coarsely grate the potatoes and pat them dry with kitchen paper. Repeat with the onions, keeping the two separate.

2 Heat the oil and butter in a frying pan over a moderate heat. Cover the base of the pan with half the potatoes. Top this with half the onions. Season.

3 Mix the cheese with the chilli powder and parsley and sprinkle evenly over the onions to cover.

4 Add the remaining onions and potatoes in the same way, finishing with a layer of potatoes. Using a fish slice press down to make a firm even surface.

5 Cook covered for 35 minutes. If you don't have a big enough lid, use kitchen foil. Pinch it round the edges to seal. Use oven gloves to avoid burning your fingers!

6 Turn the rösti over so you can brown the other side. I find the easiest method is to slide it onto a large plate. Place another plate on top. Turn them over. Remove the top plate and carefully slide the rösti back into the pan so the browned side is uppermost.

7 Cook for a further 15–20 minutes until the bottom is golden and crisp. Serve cut into wedges.

# Sweet & Sour with Cashew Nuts

*Children's Choice*

like to serve this sweet-and-sour dish with brown rice.

## Serves 2

**75g/3oz cashew nuts**
**½ tbsp cornflour**
**1 tsp caster sugar**
**2 tbsp red-wine vinegar**
**1½ tbsp soy sauce**
**1 tsp lemon juice**
**½ tbsp sesame oil**
**1 tbsp sunflower oil**
**225g/8oz carrots, peeled and cut into batons**
**150g/5oz courgettes, cut into batons**
**125g/4½oz broccoli florets, blanched**
**1 clove garlic, peeled and crushed**

## Serves 4

**175g/6oz cashew nuts**
**1 tbsp cornflour**
**2 tsp caster sugar**
**4 tbsp red-wine vinegar**
**3 tbsp soy sauce**
**2 tsp lemon juice**
**1 tbsp sesame oil**
**2 tbsp sunflower oil**
**450g/1lb carrots, peeled and cut into batons**
**275g/10oz courgettes, cut into batons**
**250g/9oz broccoli florets, blanched**
**2 cloves garlic, peeled and crushed**

1 Preheat the oven to 190°C/375°F/Gas 5. Spread the cashew nuts on a shallow baking tray and cook in the preheated oven for 10–12 minutes until golden. Leave until cool enough to handle, then roughly chop and set aside.

2 In a small bowl mix the cornflour and sugar. Add a little of the vinegar and stir to form a smooth paste. Now add the remaining vinegar along with the soy sauce, lemon juice and sesame oil. Stir well to mix.

3 Heat the oil in a large wok and stir-fry the carrots until they are just tender. Add the courgettes, broccoli and garlic cook for a further 2–3 minutes.

4 Pour over the cornflour and vinegar mixture and cook, stirring, until the mixture has thickened and is bubbling hot.

5 Remove from the heat and stir through the cashew nuts, season to taste and serve with brown rice.

# Frittata

*Low cal*

This thick omelette is packed with potatoes, beans and peppers. It can be served either on its own or with a light salad.

## Serves 2-3

175g/ 6oz new potatoes
50g/2oz green beans,
    trimmed and cut into
    5cm/2in lengths
1 tbsp olive oil
1 red onion, peeled and
    finely chopped
½ red pepper, chopped
½ orange pepper, chopped
1 clove garlic, peeled and
    crushed
75g/3oz courgettes, chopped
3 eggs
salt and freshly ground
    black pepper
50g/2oz pitted black olives
40g/1½oz Parmesan cheese,
    finely grated

## Serves 4-6

350g/12oz new potatoes
100g/4oz green beans,
    trimmed and cut into
    5cm/2in lengths
2 tbsp olive oil
1 large red onion, peeled and
    finely chopped
1 red pepper, chopped
1 orange pepper, chopped
2 cloves garlic, peeled and
    crushed
175g/6oz courgettes, chopped
6 eggs
salt and freshly ground
    black pepper
100g/4oz pitted black olives
75g/3oz Parmesan cheese,
    finely grated

1 Scrub the potatoes and cut into bite-size chunks if large. Bring a large pan of water to the boil and add the potatoes. Cook for about 10 minutes or until just tender. Add the beans and cook for a further 2 minutes, drain and set to one side.

2 Meanwhile heat the oil in a large frying pan and cook the onions until golden in places. Add the peppers and cook for 5 minutes, stirring from time to time. Add the drained potatoes and the garlic. Continue to cook, stirring from time to time, until the peppers are softened and the potatoes are starting to get golden in places.

3 Add the courgettes and beans and stir-fry for 3–4 minutes or until the courgettes are tender. Beat the eggs together and season with salt and pepper.

4 Pour the eggs over the vegetables, tilting the pan to spread them evenly through the vegetables. Sprinkle the olives over the top.

5 Preheat the grill to moderate. Cook gently on the stove top for approximately 5 minutes or until set. Sprinkle with the Parmesan cheese and place under the preheated grill for 3–4 minutes. Serve cut in wedges on its own, or with a light salad.

# casseroles and stews

# Dhal

*One Pot*

There are many variations of this recipe, and once you have cooked it a few times, you will no doubt make your own adjustments. That is the great thing about dhal – you can vary the sort of lentils used, add more or less chilli and so on.

## Serves 2

2 tbsp sunflower oil
1 large onion, peeled and
    sliced
1 green chilli, finely sliced
1 clove garlic, peeled and
    crushed
1 tsp ground cumin
1 tsp ground coriander
¼ tsp ground turmeric
½ tsp paprika
¼ tsp chilli powder (optional)
175g/6oz whole green lentils,
    washed and drained
1 x 200g/7oz can chopped
    tomatoes
salt and freshly ground
    black pepper
plain yoghurt to serve

## Serves 4

4 tbsp sunflower oil
2 large onions, peeled and
    sliced
2 green chillies, finely sliced
2 cloves garlic, peeled and
    crushed
2 tsp ground cumin
2 tsp ground coriander
½ tsp ground turmeric
1 tsp paprika
½ tsp chilli powder (optional)
350g/12oz whole green lentils,
    washed and drained
1 x 400g/14oz can chopped
    tomatoes
salt and freshly ground
    black pepper
plain yoghurt to serve

1 Heat half the oil in a large frying pan over a moderately high heat and cook half the onion and chilli until golden and crisp. Remove, using a slotted spoon, and set to one side to drain on kitchen paper.

2 Reduce the heat to moderate and add the remaining oil to the same frying pan. Cook the remaining onion and chilli along with the garlic until softened. Now stir in the spices and cook for 1–2 minutes.

3 Add the drained lentils and mix well to coat in the spiced onion mixture. Stir in the tomatoes and 600ml/1pt (1.2l/2pt) water.

4 Bring to the boil. Reduce the heat to a gentle simmer and cook for 25 minutes until the lentils are tender and the mixture is thick.

5 Remove from the heat and season to taste. Serve sprinkled with the crisp onions and chilli and a spoonful of plain yoghurt.

# Chilli

*One Pot*

If you like your chilli hotter, increase the amount of chilli that you include accordingly, but don't forget that the longer the dish cooks, the more the flavours will develop.

## Serves 2

1 tbsp oil
½ onion, peeled and chopped
1 clove garlic, peeled and
    finely chopped
½ red pepper, deseeded and
    chopped
½ green pepper, deseeded
    and chopped
½ tsp chilli powder
½ tsp dried oregano
½ tsp ground cumin
1 tbsp tomato purée
125g/5oz carrots, peeled and
    coarsely grated
125g/5oz courgettes,
    coarsely grated
½ ripe avocado
1 x 200g/7oz can chopped
    tomatoes
1 x 200g/7oz can red kidney
    beans
salt and freshly ground
    black pepper

## Serves 4

2 tbsp oil
1 onion, peeled and chopped
2 cloves garlic, peeled and
    finely chopped
1 red pepper, deseeded and
    chopped
1 green pepper, deseeded
    and chopped
1 tsp chilli powder
1 tsp dried oregano
1 tsp ground cumin
2 tbsp tomato purée
250g/9oz carrots, peeled and
    coarsely grated
250g/9oz courgettes,
    coarsely grated
1 ripe avocado
1 x 400g/14oz can chopped
    tomatoes
1 x 400g/14oz can red kidney
    beans
salt and freshly ground
    black pepper

1 Heat the oil in a large frying pan and cook the onion and garlic until softened.

2 Add the red and green pepper and continue to cook for a further 5–10 minutes until softened

3 Add the chilli powder, oregano and cumin and cook, stirring, for 1 minute.

4 Add the tomato purée, carrot and courgette and cook for 5 minutes.

5 Peel and roughly mash the avocado and add along with the tomatoes and beans. Stir in 150ml/¼pt (300ml/½pt) water. Bring gently to the boil. Simmer, covered, for 15 minutes or until thick. Season to taste and serve with rice and soured cream if desired.

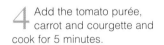

# Green Curry

*Children's Choice*

Green-curry paste is widely available from large supermarkets and well-stocked grocery shops.

## Serves 2

125g/4½oz firm tofu
1 tbsp sunflower oil
1 onion, peeled and chopped
1 small clove garlic, peeled and chopped
1–2 tbsp green-curry paste
100g/4oz green beans
100g/4oz courgettes, cut into sticks
100g/4oz broccoli florets
150ml/¼pt coconut milk
2 tbsp fresh coriander, chopped
salt and freshly ground black pepper

## Serves 4

250g/9oz firm tofu
2 tbsp sunflower oil
1 large onion, peeled and chopped
1 clove garlic, peeled and chopped
2–3 tbsp green-curry paste
200g/7oz green beans
200g/7oz courgettes, cut into sticks
200g/7oz broccoli florets
300ml/½pt coconut milk
4 tbsp fresh coriander, chopped
salt and freshly ground black pepper

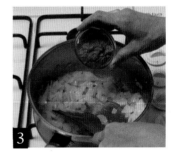

1 Pat the tofu dry with kitchen paper. Cut into small cubes.

2 Heat the oil in a large frying pan over a moderately high heat and cook the tofu until golden, turning it often. Remove, using a slotted spoon, and drain on kitchen paper.

3 Reduce the heat to moderate. Use the same pan to cook the onion and garlic until softened. Stir in the green-curry paste and cook for 1 minute.

4 Toss the prepared green beans, courgettes and broccoli florets through the onions and curry paste. Pour over the coconut milk and stir.

5 Bring gently to the boil. Reduce the heat to a gentle simmer and cover. Cook for 25 minutes, stirring from time to time. Return the tofu to the pan and cook for a further 5 minutes until piping hot.

6 Remove from the heat and stir through the coriander. Season to taste and serve over boiled rice.

# Groundnut Stew

Children's Choice

This dish can be made easily from store-cupboard and pantry ingredients.

## Serves 2

1 egg
1 tbsp sunflower oil
1 onion, peeled and
    chopped
1 small clove garlic, peeled
    and crushed
½ tsp chilli powder
1 x 200g/7oz can chopped
    tomatoes
50g/2oz soya mince
50g/2oz crunchy peanut
    butter
75ml/2½fl oz coconut milk
salt and freshly ground
    black pepper
chopped fresh coriander
    to garnish

## Serves 4

2 eggs
2 tbsp sunflower oil
1 large onion, peeled and
    chopped
1 clove garlic, peeled and
    crushed
1 tsp chilli powder
1 x 400g/14oz can chopped
    tomatoes
100g/4oz soya mince
100g/4oz crunchy peanut
    butter
150ml/¼pt coconut milk
salt and freshly ground
    black pepper
chopped fresh coriander
    to garnish

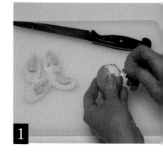

1 Bring a pan of water to the boil and cook the eggs for 10–12 minutes. Remove from the heat and drain. Cover the eggs with cold water and leave to cool before peeling and cutting into quarters. Set to one side while you make the rest of the dish.

2 In a large frying pan heat the oil over a moderate heat and cook the onion and garlic until softened.

3 Stir in the chilli powder and mix well before adding the tomatoes.

4 Sprinkle over the soya mince and stir. Cook for 1–2 minutes. Add 150ml/¼pt (300ml/½pt) water. Mix well and simmer gently for 3–4 minutes.

5 Stir in the peanut butter and coconut milk and bring gently to the boil. Reduce the heat to a gentle simmer and cook, stirring from time to time, for 10–15 minutes.

6 Remove from the heat. Season to taste and serve with the quartered hard-boiled eggs and chopped coriander.

# Lentils with Coconut Milk & Chilli

*One Pot*

A low-fat version of coconut milk is now available, so if you are watching your weight, use that. Serve with rice or naan breads.

## Serves 2

1 tbsp sunflower oil
1 onion, peeled and
   chopped
1 clove garlic, peeled and
   crushed
1cm-/½in-piece fresh root
   ginger, peeled and finely
   grated
1 red chilli, chopped (and
   deseeded if desired)
½ stick lemon grass
100g/4oz whole green lentils,
   washed and drained
200ml/7fl oz coconut milk
2 tbsp fresh coriander,
   chopped
salt and freshly ground
   black pepper
1 tbsp toasted peanuts,
   chopped

## Serves 4

2 tbsp sunflower oil
1 large onion, peeled and
   chopped
2 cloves garlic, peeled and
   crushed
2cm-/1in-piece fresh root
   ginger, peeled and finely
   grated
2 red chillies, chopped (and
   deseeded if desired)
1 stick lemon grass
200g/7oz whole green lentils,
   washed and drained
400ml/14fl oz coconut milk
4 tbsp fresh coriander,
   chopped
salt and freshly ground
   black pepper
2 tbsp toasted peanuts,
   chopped

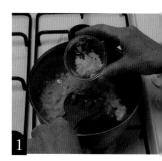

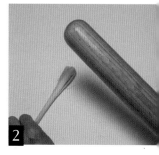

1 Heat the oil in a large pan and cook the onion until it becomes softened. Add the garlic, ginger and chillies and cook for a further 3–4 minutes.

2 Crush the lemon grass by hitting the length of it with a rolling pin.

3 Add the lemon grass and lentils to the pan and toss well to coat in the mixture.

4 Add the coconut milk and 100ml/3½fl oz (200ml/7fl oz) water. Reduce the heat to a gentle simmer and cover. Cook, stirring occasionally, for 20 minutes until the lentils are tender.

5 Remove from the heat and stir through the chopped coriander. Season to taste and serve sprinkled with toasted chopped peanuts.

# Tagine

Easy Entertaining

This dish may be hot and spicy, but you can still taste the sweetness of the dried apricots.

## Serves 2

1 tbsp olive oil
1 onion, peeled and cut into wedges
1 clove garlic, peeled and crushed
½ green pepper, deseeded and chopped
½ tsp ground cumin
¼ tsp turmeric
400g/14oz butternut squash, peeled, deseeded and chopped
1 x 200g/7oz can chopped tomatoes
150ml/¼pt vegetable stock
50g/2oz dried apricots
1 x 200g/7oz can chickpeas, rinsed and drained
½–1 tsp harissa, or to taste
salt and freshly ground black pepper

## Serves 4

2 tbsp olive oil
2 onions, peeled and cut into wedges
2 cloves garlic, peeled and crushed
1 green pepper, deseeded and chopped
1 tsp ground cumin
½ tsp turmeric
800g/1lb 12oz butternut squash, peeled, deseeded and chopped
1 x 400g/14oz can chopped tomatoes
300ml/½pt vegetable stock
100g/4oz dried apricots
1 x 400g/14oz can chickpeas, rinsed and drained
1–2 tsp harissa, or to taste
salt and freshly ground black pepper

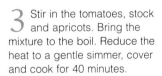

1 Heat the oil in a large saucepan and cook the onion and garlic until the onion is softened. Add the green pepper and cook for a further 3–4 minutes.

2 Stir in the cumin and turmeric and cook for 1 minute before adding the butternut squash. Stir well to coat in the spiced oil mixture.

3 Stir in the tomatoes, stock and apricots. Bring the mixture to the boil. Reduce the heat to a gentle simmer, cover and cook for 40 minutes.

4 Stir in the chick peas and harissa. Cover and cook for a further 20 minutes.

5 Remove from the heat and season lightly. Serve with couscous.

# Goulash

*Low Cal*

If you can only find regular paprika, that's fine, but if you can track down some sweet paprika for this dish, it will taste even better (and many supermarkets and delicatessens now stock a far wider range of herbs and spices than they did in the past). I do not recommend using hot paprika, however!

### Serves 2

**1 tbsp sunflower oil**
**1 large onion, peeled and**
    **chopped**
**2 large red peppers,**
    **deseeded and chopped**
**250g/9oz potatoes, peeled**
    **and cut into chunks**
**1½ tbsp paprika**
**150ml/¼pt vegetable stock**
**1 x 200g/7oz can cannellini**
    **beans, rinsed and drained**
**salt and freshly ground**
    **black pepper**

### Serves 4

**2 tbsp sunflower oil**
**2 large onions, peeled and**
    **chopped**
**4 large red peppers,**
    **deseeded and chopped**
**500g/1lb 1oz potatoes, peeled**
    **and cut into chunks**
**3 tbsp paprika**
**300ml/½pt vegetable stock**
**1 x 400g/14oz can cannellini**
    **beans, rinsed and drained**
**salt and freshly ground**
    **black pepper**

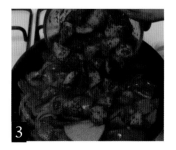

1 Heat the oil in a large frying pan and cook the onions over a moderate heat until they are tender and softened.

2 Add the chopped peppers and continue to cook for a further 10 minutes, stirring from time to time, until the peppers are soft and starting to turn golden in places.

3 Toss the chopped potatoes in the paprika to coat. Add them to the pan and cook, stirring for 2–3 minutes.

4 Stir in the stock and beans and bring gently to the boil. Now reduce the heat to a gentle simmer.

5 Cook. stirring from time to time, for 40 minutes until the mixture is thickened and the potatoes are tender and starting to break up a little.

6 Season to taste and serve with noodles and sour cream.

# Stroganoff

*Easy Entertaining*

This dish of creamy mushrooms in a brandy-and-mustard sauce goes beautifully with noodles.

### Serves 2

**25g/1oz unsalted butter**
**2 shallots, peeled and sliced**
**300g/10½oz mushrooms,**
**    cleaned and sliced**
**1½ tbsp plain flour**
**150ml/¼pt vegetable stock**
**1½ tbsp brandy**
**75ml/2½fl oz double cream**
**½ tbsp Dijon mustard**
**2 tbsp fresh parsley,**
**    chopped**
**salt and freshly ground**
**    black pepper**

### Serves 4

**50g/2oz unsalted butter**
**4 shallots, peeled and sliced**
**600g/1lb 5oz mushrooms,**
**    cleaned and sliced**
**3 tbsp plain flour**
**300ml/½pt vegetable stock**
**3 tbsp brandy**
**150ml/¼pt double cream**
**1 tbsp Dijon mustard**
**4 tbsp fresh parsley,**
**    chopped**
**salt and freshly ground**
**    black pepper**

1 Heat the butter in a large frying pan or casserole until melted. Add the shallots and cook until they are soft.

2 Add the mushrooms and cook, stirring from time to time, until tender.

3 Sprinkle over the flour and cook, stirring, for 1 minute.

4 Add about a quarter of the stock, stirring all the time until thickened. Continue adding the stock in this way until it is all incorporated, stirring well to ensure that the mixture is smooth and thickened.

5 Simmer gently for 5 minutes, then stir in the brandy. Now add the double cream and mustard, stirring to mix.

6 Remove from the heat and sprinkle over the chopped parsley, season to taste and serve.

# Rich Autumn Casserole with Cheese & Chive Dumplings

*One Pot*

I sometimes make this the day before up to the end of step 3, then cool it and place in the fridge until the next day when I am ready to finish it. I think that the casserole benefits from the length of time it has to mature in flavour. Just make sure it is piping hot before you add the dumplings. The dumplings will not freeze well but you can easily freeze the rest of the casserole if you wish.

## Serves 2-4

1 tbsp oil
1 onion, peeled and cut into thin wedges
1 large leek, washed and sliced
1 clove garlic, peeled and crushed
1 large carrot, peeled and cut into thick slices
1 large parsnip, peeled and cut into thick slices
150g/5oz swede, peeled and cut into chunks
200g/7oz black-eyed beans, rinsed and drained
1 tsp mixed, dried herbs
1 tbsp tomato purée
300ml/½pt vegetable stock
150ml/¼pt red wine
salt and freshly ground black pepper
50g/2oz self-raising flour
25g/1oz vegetable suet
15g/½oz Parmesan cheese, finely grated
15g/½oz mature Cheddar cheese, grated
½ tbsp fresh chives, finely chopped
1 tbsp fresh parsley, finely chopped

## Serves 4-8

2 tbsp oil
1 large onion, peeled and cut into thin wedges
2 large leeks, washed and sliced
2 cloves garlic, peeled and crushed
2 large carrots, peeled and cut into thick slices
2 large parsnips, peeled and cut into thick slices
300g/10½oz swede, peeled and cut into chunks
400g/14oz black-eyed beans, rinsed and drained
2 tsp mixed, dried herbs
2 tbsp tomato purée
600ml/1pt vegetable stock
300ml/½pt red wine
salt and freshly ground black pepper
100g/4oz self-raising flour
50g/2oz vegetable suet
25g/1oz Parmesan cheese, finely grated
25g/1oz mature Cheddar cheese, grated
1 tbsp fresh chives, finely chopped
2 tbsp fresh parsley, finely chopped

1 Preheat the oven to 180°C/350°F/Gas 4. In a large frying pan heat the oil over a moderate heat and cook the onion until softened. Add the leeks and garlic and continue to cook for a further 5 minutes, stirring from to time. Using a slotted spoon transfer to a large casserole with a well-fitting lid.

2 Add the carrots, parsnips and swede to the frying pan and stir-fry quickly for 3–4 minutes or until they start to get a little golden in places. Add these to the casserole dish with the beans and stir.

3 Sprinkle over the mixed herbs and stir in the tomato purée. Pour over the stock and wine and season to taste. Cover and cook in the preheated oven for 1 hour.

4 After approximately 50 minutes make the dumplings. In a bowl mix the flour, suet and cheeses together. Add the herbs and a little salt and pepper. Stir. Add enough cold water to form a stiff dough. Divide the mixture into 4 (8) and shape into rough balls. If the mixture is a little sticky it may be easier to shape the dumplings with damp hands.

5 Remove the casserole from the oven and place the dumplings on the surface. Cover and return to the oven for 15 minutes. Serve as it is or with chunks of crusty bread or boiled potatoes.

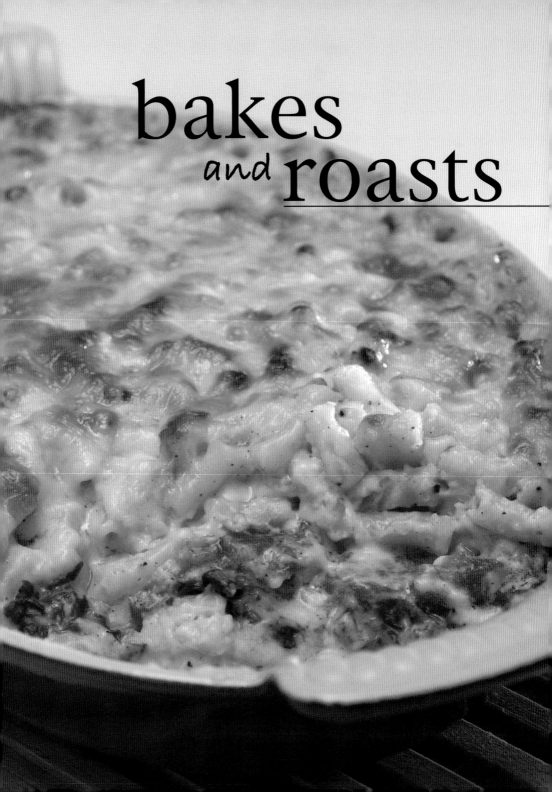

# bakes
### and roasts

# Red-cabbage & Chickpea Bake

*One Pot*

This dish tastes even better if it is made the day before it is due to be eaten. Simply prepare it to the end of step 4, let it cool and then chill it in the fridge until you are ready to resume cooking. The next day, start by heating it until it is bubbling hot, then continue with the recipe.

## Serves 2-3

½ medium-sized red cabbage
25g/1oz butter
½ tbsp olive oil
100g/4oz baby onions, peeled
1 clove garlic, peeled and
  crushed
125g/4½oz cooking apple,
  peeled and sliced
150ml/¼pt red wine
50ml/3½ tbsp red wine vinegar
1 heaped tbsp soft,
  dark-brown sugar
1 tsp dried thyme
4 thick slices French bread
1 x 200g/7oz can chickpeas,
  rinsed and drained
salt and freshly ground
  black pepper

## Serves 4-6

1 medium-sized red cabbage
50g/2oz butter
1 tbsp olive oil
200g/7oz baby onions, peeled
2 cloves garlic, peeled and
  crushed
250g/9oz cooking apple,
  peeled and sliced
300ml/½pt red wine
100ml/3½fl oz red wine
  vinegar
2 heaped tbsp soft,
  dark-brown sugar
2 tsp dried thyme
8 thick slices French bread
1 x 400g/14oz can chickpeas,
  rinsed and drained
salt and freshly ground
  black pepper

1 Remove any tough outer leaves from the cabbage and discard. Using a large sharp knife cut the cabbage in half from top to bottom. Remove the tough core and discard. Finely shred and set to one side.

2 Preheat the oven to 170°C/325°F/Gas 3. Heat half the butter and all the oil in a large ovenproof casserole. Add the baby onions and cook over a moderate heat until they start to brown.

6

3 Stir in half the garlic and the apple and cook for 1–2 minutes. Add the shredded cabbage and cook, stirring until well mixed.

4 Pour over the wine and vinegar. Sprinkle with the sugar and herbs and stir well to mix. Cover with a well-fitting lid and place in the oven for 1 hour.

5 Mix the remaining butter with the garlic and spread over the bread slices.

6 Remove the casserole from the oven and stir through the chick peas and season to taste. Top with the buttered bread and return to the oven uncovered for 15 minutes. Serve.

# Stuffed Aubergines

*Easy Entertaining*

Although aubergines are now available all year round, they are generally cheaper during the summer, making this an economical, as well as a delicious, warm-weather dish.

### Serves 2

1 large aubergine
salt
2 tbsp olive oil
1 onion, peeled and chopped
1 small clove garlic, peeled and crushed
1 celery stalk
2 large tomatoes, peeled and chopped
½ tbsp tomato purée
¼ tsp allspice
1 tbsp fresh parsley, chopped
25g/1oz pitted black olives
freshly ground black pepper
½ tsp sugar
½ lemon, juiced
75g/3oz mozzarella, drained and sliced
basil for garnishing

### Serves 4

2 large aubergines
salt
4 tbsp olive oil
1 large onion, peeled and chopped
1 clove garlic, peeled and crushed
2 celery stalks
4 large tomatoes, peeled and chopped
1 tbsp tomato purée
½ tsp allspice
3 tbsp fresh parsley, chopped
50g/2oz pitted black olives
freshly ground black pepper
1 tsp sugar
1 lemon, juiced
150g/5oz mozzarella, drained and sliced
basil for garnishing

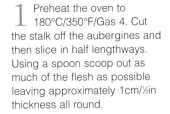

**1**

1 Preheat the oven to 180°C/350°F/Gas 4. Cut the stalk off the aubergines and then slice in half lengthways. Using a spoon scoop out as much of the flesh as possible leaving approximately 1cm/½in thickness all round.

2 Roughly chop the flesh and reserve. Sprinkle the insides of the aubergine skins liberally with salt and place them cut side down on a plate for about 30 minutes.

3 Heat 3–4 tbsp of the oil in a large frying pan and cook the onions over a moderate heat for 5 minutes until softened. Add the garlic and celery and cook for a further 3–4 minutes.

4 Stir in the tomatoes and chopped aubergine flesh and cook for 10 minutes to soften.

5 Add the tomato purée, allspice, parsley and olives. Season to taste. Remove from the heat.

6 Rinse the aubergine skins thoroughly and pat dry with kitchen paper. Place in a shallow ovenproof dish. Divide the mixture between the aubergine skins.

7 Mix the lemon juice and sugar with 150ml/¼pt (300ml/½pt) boiling water and the remaining oil and pour around the aubergines, being careful not to pour it into the aubergines. Cover loosely with tinfoil, pinching round the edges to seal. Bake in the preheated oven for 45 minutes. Remove the foil and top each aubergine with the mozzarella slices. Return to the oven for a further 15 minutes. Serve garnished with basil.

# Luxury Nut Loaf

Easy Entertaining

Nut loaf, accompanied by potatoes and vegetables, makes a lovely main course. Ready-peeled chestnuts sold in vacuum-sealed packs will make this dish much easier to prepare.

### Serves 6-8

**175g/6oz butter**
**1 large onion, peeled and chopped**
**100g/4oz raw cashew nuts**
**100g/4oz peeled chestnuts, roughly chopped**
**225g/8oz fresh brown breadcrumbs**
**2 eggs, beaten**
**4 tbsp single cream**
**salt and freshly ground black pepper**
**100g/4oz shitake mushrooms, finely chopped**
**1 clove garlic, peeled and crushed**
**1 lemon**
**1 tsp dried thyme**
**3 tbsp fresh parsley, chopped**

1 Lightly grease and line a 23 x 12.5 x 7.5cm/9 x 5 x 3in loaf tin. Preheat the oven to 200°C/400°F/Gas 5.

2 Heat half the butter in a large frying pan and cook the onions until softened.

3 Finely chop the cashew nuts in a food processor or blender. Place in a large bowl with the chestnuts and half the breadcrumbs. Add the onions and any butter from the pan. Stir in the beaten eggs and cream. Season to taste.

4 Heat the remaining butter in the frying pan and cook the chopped mushrooms and garlic until softened. Finely grate the zest from the lemon and squeeze the juice. Add to the cooked mushrooms.

5 Add the remaining breadcrumbs, thyme and parsley. Season to taste.

6 Press half of the nut mix into the base of the tin. Top with the mushroom mix, then the remaining nut mix. Level with the back of a spoon.

7 Cover with tinfoil and bake in the preheated oven for 45 minutes. Remove the foil. Return to the oven for 15 minutes. Leave to stand for 5 minutes before turning out.

# Mushroom & Stilton Wellington

*Easy Entertaining*

Flaky puff-pastry wrapped around a large, juicy mushroom and rich Stilton makes this a most impressive dish to serve on a special occasion. Serve the pastry parcels with steamed vegetables or a green salad.

## Serves 2

- 2 large field mushrooms, measuring about 12.5cm/5in across
- ½ tbsp oil
- 25g/1oz butter
- 2 shallots, peeled and chopped
- 2 tbsp fresh parsley, chopped
- 25g/1oz fresh brown breadcrumbs
- 250g/9oz puff-pastry
- 50g/2oz Stilton cheese, crumbled
- 1 egg, beaten
- salt and freshly ground black pepper

## Serves 4

- 4 large field mushrooms, measuring about 12.5cm/5in across
- 1 tbsp oil
- 50g/2oz butter
- 4 shallots, peeled and chopped
- 4 tbsp fresh parsley, chopped
- 50g/2oz fresh brown breadcrumbs
- 500g/1lb 2oz puff-pastry
- 100g/4oz Stilton cheese, thinly sliced
- 1 egg, beaten
- salt and freshly ground black pepper

1 Preheat the oven to 200°C/400°F/Gas 6. Wipe the mushrooms with a damp cloth. Remove the stalk and chop. Brush the mushrooms with oil. Set aside.

2 Heat the butter in a frying pan and cook the shallots and chopped mushroom stalks until tender. Remove from the heat and stir in the parsley and breadcrumbs.

3 Divide the pastry into 2 (4) and roll out each piece on

a lightly floured board until large enough to wrap round a mushroom. Place each mushroom on a piece of pastry. Divide the breadcrumb mixture between them. Top each with some of the Stilton.

4 Brush the pastry edges with beaten egg. Draw the pastry over the mushrooms, pinching the edges together to seal. Place on a lightly oiled baking tray. Cook in the preheated oven for 25 minutes until golden and crisp.

# Beans on Toast with a Twist

*Children's Choice*

This is a new version of an old theme.

## Serves 2

½ tbsp sunflower oil
1 small onion, peeled and finely chopped
1 small clove garlic, peeled and crushed
1 x 200g/7oz can black-eyed beans, rinsed and drained
1 x 200g/7oz can cannellini beans, rinsed and drained
150ml/¼pt passata
1 tbsp tomato purée
1 tbsp tomato ketchup
4 thick slices bread
½ tbsp Dijon mustard
50g/2oz mature Cheddar cheese, grated
salt and freshly ground black pepper

## Serves 4

1 tbsp sunflower oil
1 onion, peeled and finely chopped
1 clove garlic, peeled and crushed
1 x 400g/14oz can black-eyed beans, rinsed and drained
1 x 400g/14oz can cannellini beans, rinsed and drained
300ml/½pt passata
2 tbsp tomato purée
2 tbsp tomato ketchup
8 thick slices bread
1 tbsp Dijon mustard
100g/4oz mature Cheddar cheese, grated
salt and freshly ground black pepper

1 In a large saucepan heat the oil over a moderate heat and cook the onion and garlic for 3–4 minutes until softened. Add the drained beans, passata, purée and ketchup. Stir well to mix. Bring gently to the boil. Reduce the heat to a gentle simmer and cook for 25 minutes, stirring from time to time until thickened. Preheat the oven to 200°C/400°F/Gas 6.

2 Cut a disc out of the centre of 2 (4) of the slices of bread. Divide the mustard between the remaining slices of bread and spread to the edges. Sprinkle over the cheese and top with the frame of bread. Place on a baking sheet and cook in the preheated oven for 10 minutes until golden brown and the cheese has melted.

3 To serve place a cheesy toast on each plate and spoon the beans into the cut-out space. Season to taste and serve.

# Leek & Cheese Soufflés

*Easy Entertaining*

These soufflés should be served straight from the oven, while they're golden and risen.

### Serves 2

**butter for greasing**
**15g/½oz Parmesan cheese,**
    **finely grated**
**½ tbsp sunflower oil**
**1½ large leeks, washed and**
    **finely sliced**
**1 small clove garlic, peeled**
    **and crushed**
**3 eggs**
**2 tbsp single cream**
**25g/1oz wholemeal**
    **breadcrumbs**
**50g/2oz Cheddar cheese,**
    **grated**
**½ tsp dried mixed herbs**
**salt and freshly ground**
    **black pepper**

### Serves 4

**butter for greasing**
**25g/1oz Parmesan cheese,**
    **finely grated**
**1 tbsp sunflower oil**
**3 large leeks, washed and**
    **finely sliced**
**1 clove garlic, peeled and**
    **crushed**
**6 eggs**
**4 tbsp single cream**
**50g/2oz wholemeal**
    **breadcrumbs**
**100g/4oz Cheddar cheese,**
    **grated**
**1 tsp mixed herbs**
**salt and freshly ground**
    **black pepper**

1 Preheat the oven to 200°C/400°F/Gas 6. Lightly grease 2 (4) ovenproof 450ml/¾pt bowls. Coat with the Parmesan reserving any that does not stick to the sides. Set to one side.

2 Heat the oil in a large frying pan and cook the leeks and garlic for 10 minutes until softened. Leave to cool a little.

3 Separate the eggs. Add the cream, breadcrumbs, Cheddar, mixed herbs and any remaining Parmesan to the egg yolks and beat.

4 Stir in the cooked leeks and beat again. Season with salt and freshly ground black pepper.

5 Whisk the egg whites until they form soft peaks. Using a large metal spoon gently fold the egg whites through the leek mixture.

6 Divide the mixture between the prepared bowls. Bake in the preheated oven for 15–20 minutes until golden and springy to the touch. Serve.

# Baked Onions

*Low Cal*

Years ago, baked onions were a popular dish. These are stuffed with a mixture of breadcrumbs and mushrooms before being topped with cheese.

### Serves 2

**2 large onions**
**½ tbsp olive oil**
**1 small clove garlic, peeled and chopped**
**100g/4oz mushrooms, cleaned and chopped**
**½ lemon**
**75g/3oz fresh breadcrumbs**
**1 tbsp fresh parsley, chopped**
**salt and freshly ground black pepper**
**40g/1½oz mature Cheddar cheese, grated**

### Serves 4

**4 large onions**
**1 tbsp olive oil**
**1 clove garlic, peeled and chopped**
**200g/7oz mushrooms, cleaned and chopped**
**1 lemon**
**150g/5oz fresh breadcrumbs**
**2 tbsp fresh parsley, chopped**
**salt and freshly ground black pepper**
**75g/3oz mature Cheddar cheese, grated**

1 Preheat the oven to 190°C/375°F/Gas 5. Remove the root end from the onions, they should now stand upright. Wrap loosely in tinfoil and place on a baking tray.

2 Cook in the preheated oven for 35 minutes. Leave until cool enough to handle. Remove the papery outer skins and discard.

3 Cut the top off the onions about ⅓ down. Scoop out the inside of the onion and finely chop. Set the outer shell to one side while you prepare the filling.

4 Heat the oil in a large frying pan and cook the chopped onion until starting to turn golden in places. Add the garlic and mushrooms and cook until tender.

5 Finely grate the zest from the lemon and squeeze the juice. Stir the zest and juice into the onion and mushroom and cook for 1 minute. Remove from the heat, add the breadcrumbs and parsley, season to taste.

6 Use this mixture to stuff the onions, be careful not to split the skins. Sprinkle over the cheese and wrap each loosely in lightly greased foil. Pour 1 tbsp water around each onion, then scrunch up the foil to seal. Bake for 40 minutes. Open the foil and return to the oven for 10 minutes. Serve.

# Baby Bubble & Squeak with Boston Beans

*Children's Choice*

If you have any leftover vegetables, bubble and squeak may be the perfect way of using them up. Bubble and squeak is traditionally made with cabbage and potatoes, but I often add carrots, swede and even broccoli.

| Serves 2 | Serves 4 |
|---|---|
| 250g/9oz potatoes, peeled and cut into chunks | 500g/1lb 2oz potatoes, peeled and cut into chunks |
| 1 tbsp double cream | 2 tbsp double cream |
| 125g/4½oz green cabbage, shredded | 250g/9oz green cabbage, shredded |
| 15g/½oz butter | 25g/1oz butter |
| 3 spring onions, cleaned and thinly sliced | 6 spring onions, cleaned and thinly sliced |
| salt and freshly ground black pepper | salt and freshly ground black pepper |
| ½ tsp oil | 1 tsp oil |
| ½ small onion, peeled and very finely chopped | 1 small onion, peeled and very finely chopped |
| 1 clove garlic, peeled and crushed | 2 cloves garlic, peeled and crushed |
| 1 x 200g/7oz can baked beans | 1 x 400g/14oz can baked beans |
| 1 x 100g/4oz can chopped tomatoes | 1 x 200g/7oz can chopped tomatoes |
| 1 tbsp brown sauce | 2 tbsp brown sauce |
| ½ tbsp English mustard | 1 tbsp English mustard |
| ½ tbsp soft, dark-brown sugar | 1 tbsp soft, dark-brown sugar |
| ½ tbsp vinegar | 1 tbsp vinegar |
| ½ tbsp tomato purée | 1 tbsp tomato purée |

1 Preheat the oven to 200°C/ 400°F /Gas 6. Cook the potatoes in a large pan of boiling water for 10–15 minutes until tender. Drain thoroughly and mash with the cream. Cook the cabbage in a large pan of boiling water for 5–8 minutes or until just tender. Drain thoroughly and add to the mashed potato, stirring well to mix.

2 In a small frying pan heat the butter, then add the spring onions and cook for 3–4 minutes until softened. Add to the cabbage mixture along with any butter that may remain in the pan. Season to taste.

3 Divide the mixture into 4 (8) and place on a lightly greased baking sheet in rough piles, flattening slightly and then roughing up a little with a fork. Place in the preheated oven and bake for 20–25 minutes until golden in places and starting to crisp.

4 Meanwhile make the beans. In a saucepan heat the oil over a moderate heat and cook the onion until it is softened. Add the garlic and cook for a further 3 minutes.

5 Stir in the remaining ingredients and bring gently to the boil. Reduce the heat to a gentle simmer and continue to cook until the mixture has thickened, stirring from time to time. Season to taste and serve with the bubble and squeak.

# Spinach & Goat's-cheese Pizza

*Children's Choice*

Making your own pizza dough produces a very crisp base, and really isn't that difficult.

### Serves 12

**125g/5oz white-bread flour**
**1 pinch sugar**
**¼ tsp salt**
**½ tsp dried, easy-action yeast**
**1 tbsp olive oil**
**50g/2oz spinach**
**50g/2oz cherry tomatoes**
**50g/2oz goat's cheese**
**coarse cornmeal or polenta**
**salt and freshly ground**
    **black pepper**

### Serves 24

**250g/9oz white-bread flour**
**¼ tsp sugar**
**½ tsp salt**
**1 tsp dried, easy-action yeast**
**2 tbsp olive oil**
**100g/4oz spinach**
**100g/4oz cherry tomatoes**
**100g/4oz goat's cheese**
**coarse cornmeal or polenta**
**salt and freshly ground**
    **black pepper**

1 Sift the flour into a mixing bowl. Add the sugar and salt and stir to mix. Sprinkle over the yeast and mix.

2 Stir half of the olive oil into 75ml/5 tbsp (150ml/¼pt) tepid water. Make a hollow in the flour and pour in the water and oil mix, drawing the flour in from the sides to make a smooth dough. Turn out onto a lightly floured surface and knead for 10 minutes until the dough is smooth and springy to the touch. Return to the mixing bowl and cover with cling film. Leave in a warm place for 1–2 hours or until the dough has doubled in size.

3
3 Meanwhile wash the spinach and shake to remove as much of the water as possible. Roughly shred using a large sharp knife. Place in a saucepan and heat, stirring, until it just starts to wilt. Drain thoroughly and set to one side.

4 Halve the cherry tomatoes and thinly slice the goat's cheese.

5 When the dough is puffy and double in size, preheat the oven to 240°C/475°F/Gas 9. Lightly oil a baking sheet and sprinkle with the cornmeal.

6 Remove the dough from the bowl and knead briefly on a floured surface. Now roll and stretch into a large round 35cm/14in. Place on the prepared baking sheet.

7 Sprinkle over the prepared spinach and tomatoes. Drizzle over the remaining olive oil. Top with the slices of goats cheese and bake in the preheated oven for 8–10 minutes. Serve.

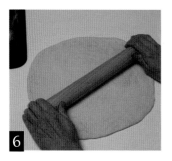
6

# Meadow Pie

*Low Cal*

There was much debate in my house about what this dish should be called as it is loosely based on shepherd's pie, but obviously without the meat. After a lot of discussion, and even more eating, we finally came up with meadow pie.

### Serves 2-4

300g/10½oz potatoes, peeled
    and cut into chunks
45ml/3 tbsp milk
15g/½oz butter
1 tbsp wholegrain mustard
salt and freshly ground
    black pepper
1 tbsp oil
1 small onion, peeled and
    chopped
100g/4oz carrots, peeled
    and diced
1 large stick celery, washed
    and chopped
100g/4oz whole green lentils,
    washed and drained
1 x 200g/7oz can chopped
    tomatoes
1 tsp yeast extract
75ml/5 tbsp vegetable stock
1 tsp dried thyme

### Serves 4-8

600g/1lb 5oz potatoes,
    peeled and cut into
    chunks
100ml/3½fl oz milk
25g/1oz butter
2 tbsp wholegrain mustard
salt and freshly ground
    black pepper
2 tbsp oil
1 onion, peeled and chopped
225g/8oz carrots, peeled
    and diced
3 sticks celery, washed and
    chopped
225g/8oz whole green lentils,
    washed and drained
1 x 400g/14oz can chopped
    tomatoes
2 tsp yeast extract
150ml/¼pt vegetable stock
1 tsp dried thyme

1 Cook the potatoes in a large pan of boiling water for 12–15 minutes or until tender. Drain thoroughly and mash with the milk, butter and mustard. Season to taste. Set to one side until ready to use.

2 Preheat the oven to 190°C/375°F/Gas 5. Heat the oil in a large frying pan and cook the onion until golden. Add the carrots and celery and continue to cook, stirring from time to time, for 5 minutes.

3 Add the lentils, tomatoes, yeast extract and vegetable stock, stirring well to mix. Bring gently to the boil. Sprinkle over the thyme and continue to cook at a gentle simmer for 10 minutes. Check the lentils to make sure they are tender. If they are still not tender cook them for a little longer, adding a little water if the mixture is looking too dry. Remove from the heat and season to taste.

4 Spoon the mixture into a large ovenproof dish. Spoon over the mashed potatoes, roughing up the surface with a fork. Bake in the preheated oven for 25 minutes until the top is golden in places and it is piping hot. Serve.

# Porcini & Rocket Roulade

*Easy Entertaining*

A roulade makes an impressive centrepiece for any dinner party. This one could also be sliced thinly and served as part of a buffet, or even as a starter or light lunch teamed with a salad, in which case it would feed 8–10 people.

*Serves 4-6*

**15g/½oz dried porcini mushrooms**
**50g/2oz plain flour, sifted, plus a little extra for dusting**
**25g/1oz Parmesan cheese, finely grated**
**50g/2oz butter**
**100g/4oz rocket, roughly chopped**
**1 clove garlic, peeled and chopped**
**300ml/½pt milk**
**4 medium-sized eggs**
**salt and freshly ground black pepper**
**75g/3oz garlic-and-herb soft cheese**
**150g/5oz ricotta cheese**

1 Place the porcini in a small bowl and pour over 150ml/¼pt boiling water. Leave to stand for 30 minutes. Now strain through a fine mesh sieve or muslin, reserving the liquid. Finely chop the porcini and set to one side.

2 Grease and line a 23 x 33cm/9 x 13in tin with baking parchment. Lightly dust the base with a little flour and 2 tbsp of the Parmesan. Preheat the oven to 200°C/400°F/Gas 6.

3 Heat the butter in a saucepan and cook the porcini for 2–3 minutes. Add the rocket and garlic and cook for 2 minutes. Sprinkle over the flour and cook, stirring, for 1 minute. Remove briefly from the heat. Add the reserved porcini liquid and milk, whisking well to combine. Return the pan to the heat and continue to cook until the mixture comes to the boil stirring all the time. Remove from the heat.

4 Separate the eggs and add the yolks one at a time to the rocket mixture, beating well between each addition. Stir in the remaining Parmesan and season with salt and freshly ground black pepper.

5 Whisk the egg whites to soft peak stage. Use a large metal spoon to fold them into the rocket mixture. Pour into the prepared tin and gently level with a palette knife or the back of a spoon. Bake in the preheated oven for about 15 minutes, but check it after 12 minutes. It needs to be just se

6 Meanwhile beat the soft cheese with the ricotta and season with black pepper

7 Remove the roulade from the oven and turn onto a clean, slightly damp tea towel. Spread the cheese mixture over the roulade and then use the tea towel to roll up, enclosing the filling. Serve cut in thick slices with salad.

# Stuffed Peppers

*Easy Entertaining*

The natural sugars in the peppers caramelise as they roast, resulting in a mouth-watering sweetness.

## Serves 2

2 large peppers
50g/2oz brown rice
½ tbsp olive oil
1 small onion, peeled and
    chopped
1 small clove garlic, peeled
    and crushed
75g/3oz mushrooms,
    chopped
1 x 100g/4oz can chopped
    tomatoes
½ tbsp tomato purée
½ tsp dried oregano
½ tbsp fresh parsley, chopped
salt and freshly ground
    black pepper
50g/2oz mature Cheddar
    cheese, grated

## Serves 4

4 large peppers
75g/3oz brown rice
1 tbsp olive oil
1 onion, peeled and
    chopped
1 clove garlic, peeled and
    crushed
175g/6oz mushrooms,
    chopped
1 x 200g/7oz can chopped
    tomatoes
1 tbsp tomato purée
1 tsp dried oregano
1 tbsp fresh parsley, chopped
salt and freshly ground
    black pepper
100g/4oz mature Cheddar
    cheese, grated

1 Preheat the oven to 190°C/375°F/Gas 5. Halve the peppers and deseed them, then place in a roasting tray.

2 Cook the brown rice in a pan of boiling water until it is tender, then drain thoroughly.

3 Heat the oil in a frying pan and cook the onion and garlic until golden. Add the mushrooms and stir. Cook for 5 minutes until softened.

4 Add the tomatoes, purée and oregano. Bring to the boil and simmer for 10 minutes or until the mixture thickens. Remove from heat, stir in the rice and parsley and season.

5 Divide the rice mixture between the peppers. Sprinkle over the grated cheese. Cover with foil and place in the oven for 25 minutes. Remove the foil and return to the oven for 15 minutes until the cheese is melted. Serve.

# Pasta Crumble

*Children's Choice*

This pasta dish, with its crunchy cheese-and-breadcrumb topping, is a popular midweek meal in my house.

## Serves 2

**175g/6oz penne pasta**
**½ tbsp olive oil**
**1 small onion, peeled and chopped**
**1 small clove garlic, peeled and crushed**
**½ green pepper, deseeded and chopped**
**1 carrot, peeled and grated**
**1 x 200g/7oz can chopped tomatoes**
**salt and freshly ground black pepper**
**60g/2½oz fresh brown breadcrumbs**
**60g/2½oz mature Cheddar cheese, grated**

## Serves 4

**350g/12oz penne pasta**
**1 tbsp olive oil**
**1 onion, peeled and chopped**
**1 clove garlic, peeled and crushed**
**1 green pepper, deseeded and chopped**
**1 large carrot, peeled and grated**
**1 x 400g/14oz can chopped tomatoes**
**salt and freshly ground black pepper**
**150g/5oz fresh brown breadcrumbs**
**150g/5oz mature Cheddar cheese, grated**

1 Bring a large pan of water to the boil and cook the pasta according to the manufacturers instructions.

2 Heat the oil in a large frying pan and cook the onion until softened.

3 Add the garlic and green pepper. Cook, stirring, for 5–8 minutes until the pepper is softened. Preheat the oven to 200°C/400°F/Gas 6.

4 Stir in the carrot and cook, stirring, for 1–2 minutes.

Add the tomatoes and bring to the boil. Reduce the heat to a gentle simmer and cook for 10 minutes until thickened.

5 Stir the tomato mixture through the drained pasta and season to taste. Pile the mixture into a large, shallow, ovenproof dish. Mix the breadcrumbs and cheese together and sprinkle in a thick layer over the pasta. Bake in the preheated oven for 15–20 minutes until the top is golden and crisp. Serve.

# Macaroni-cheese Layer

*Children's Choice*

In this dish, macaroni cheese is layered with spinach and tomatoes.

### Serves 2

125g/4½oz macaroni pasta
75g/3oz young spinach
100g/4oz tomatoes
25g/1oz butter
25g/1oz plain flour
300ml/½pt milk
1 pinch cayenne pepper
75g/3oz mature Cheddar
   cheese, grated
salt and freshly ground
   black pepper

### Serves 4

250g/9oz macaroni pasta
175g/6oz young spinach
200g/7oz tomatoes
50g/2oz butter
50g/2oz plain flour
600ml/1pt milk
1 pinch cayenne pepper
175g/6oz mature Cheddar
   cheese, grated
salt and freshly ground
   black pepper

1 Bring a large pan of water to the boil and cook the macaroni according to the manufacturer's instructions. Drain.

2 Wash the spinach and roughly chop. Place in a large saucepan and cook, stirring, until it has wilted. Drain in a colander, squeezing out as much water as you can. Finely slice the tomatoes.

3 Preheat the oven to 200°C/400°F/Gas 6. Melt the butter in a large saucepan. Stir in the flour with a wooden spoon and cook, stirring, for 1 minute. Add about ¼ of the milk, stirring well until smooth. Add the milk in this way until it

has all been incorporated and you have a smooth sauce.

4 Stir in the cayenne pepper, 100g/4oz of the cheese and the drained macaroni. Season to taste.

5 In a lightly greased large ovenproof dish spoon half of the macaroni mixture, levelling with the back of a spoon. Cover with spinach.

6 Add the sliced tomatoes followed by the remaining macaroni mixture. Sprinkle with the remaining cheese and bake in the oven for 15–20 minutes until the cheese is golden and bubbling. Serve.

# Layered Vegetable Cake

*Easy Entertaining*

The first time that I made this, it seemed as though everyone was coming back for seconds! I have since found that it reheats well if it is wrapped in tinfoil and placed in a moderately hot oven for 20 minutes until it is piping hot.

## Serves 6-8

butter
100g/4oz fresh brown breadcrumbs
75g/3oz mature Cheddar cheese, coarsely grated
2 tbsp fresh chives, chopped
2 tbsp fresh parsley, chopped
2 cloves garlic, finely chopped
salt and freshly ground black pepper
325g/11oz potatoes, peeled
325g/11oz parsnips, peeled
1 large turnip, peeled
325g/11oz sweet potatoes, peeled
325g/11oz swede, peeled
2 eggs
300ml/½pt vegetable stock
100ml/3fl oz single cream

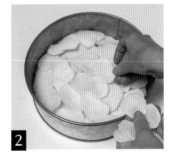

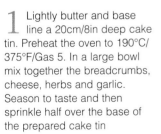

1 Lightly butter and base line a 20cm/8in deep cake tin. Preheat the oven to 190°C/375°F/Gas 5. In a large bowl mix together the breadcrumbs, cheese, herbs and garlic. Season to taste and then sprinkle half over the base of the prepared cake tin

2 Slice all the vegetables as thinly as possible. This is best done on a mandolin or in a food processor with a thin cutting disc. However, if you don't have one use a sharp knife and try to get them all a similar thickness. Now start by placing a layer of the potatoes in the bottom of the prepared tin, followed by a layer of parsnips. Top this with a layer of turnip, followed by sweet potato and then swede. Season lightly every few layers.

**4**

3 Sprinkle over half of the remaining breadcrumb mixture and then repeat the whole process again. Now top with the remaining breadcrumb mixture.

4 Beat together the eggs, stock and cream. Season. Pour this mixture evenly over the layered vegetables. Cover with foil, pinching round the edges to seal.

5 Bake in the preheated oven for 1 hour. Remove the foil and return to the oven for a further 30 minutes. Preheat the grill to high.

6 Turn out onto a heatproof plate. Remove the lining paper and discard. Place under the hot grill for 4–5 minutes until crisp and golden. Serve cut in wedges.

# rice, pasta and noodles

# Butternut-squash Risotto

*One Pot*

To serve this risotto as a starter, halve the quantities specified below. This rice dish tastes especially delicious when served with a light salad or some steamed vegetables.

## Serves 2

**225g/8oz butternut squash**
**½ tbsp olive oil**
**25g/1oz butter**
**2 shallots, peeled and finely chopped**
**500ml/18fl oz vegetable stock**
**150g/5oz arborio rice**
**25g/1oz Parmesan cheese, finely grated**
**salt and freshly ground black pepper**

## Serves 4

**450g/1lb butternut squash**
**1 tbsp olive oil**
**50g/2oz butter**
**4 shallots, peeled and finely chopped**
**1l/1¾pt vegetable stock**
**300g/10½oz arborio rice**
**50g/2oz Parmesan cheese, finely grated**
**salt and freshly ground black pepper**

1 Peel and deseed the butternut squash and cut into small chunks. Heat the oil and half the butter in a large saucepan. Add the shallots and cook over a moderate heat until they become transparent and softened. Place the stock in a saucepan, bring to the boil, then reduce the heat to a very gentle simmer. Cover.

2 Stir the butternut squash into the onions and cook for 4–5 minutes. Now add the rice and stir well to coat in the mixture, cook for 1–2 minutes. Now add 3–4 ladles of the hot stock to the rice mixture, stirring well to mix. Cook, stirring gently, until the liquid has almost been absorbed. Add another 3–4 ladles of the hot stock.

3 Continue cooking in this way until the mixture is thick and creamy and the rice is tender but not soft – risotto should have a little 'bite' to it. You may not need all the hot stock, just keeping adding it until the risotto is to your liking.

4 Remove from the heat add the remaining butter and the Parmesan, stirring quickly to mix. Season with salt and freshly ground black pepper to taste and serve.

# Red-onion & Rosemary Risotto

Easy Entertaining

Risottos take a little time and patience to cook, but the result is well worth the effort required.

## Serves 2

**225g/8oz red onions**
**1 tbsp olive oil**
**500ml/18fl oz vegetable stock**
**1 tbsp fresh rosemary,**
    **chopped**
**½ tbsp balsamic vinegar**
**150g/5oz arborio rice**
**15g/½oz butter**
**75g/3oz mozzarella cheese,**
    **drained and diced**
**salt and freshly ground**
    **black pepper**

## Serves 4

**450g/1lb red onions**
**2 tbsp olive oil**
**1l/1¾pt vegetable stock**
**2 tbsp fresh rosemary,**
    **chopped**
**1 tbsp balsamic vinegar**
**300g/10½oz arborio rice**
**25g/1oz butter**
**150g/5oz mozzarella cheese,**
    **drained and diced**
**salt and freshly ground**
    **black pepper**

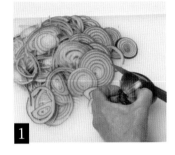

1 Peel and finely slice the red onions. Heat the oil in a large saucepan. Add the onions and cook until they are softened. Place the stock in a saucepan, bring to the boil, then reduce the heat to a very gentle simmer, cover.

2 Stir the rosemary and vinegar into the onions and cook for 1–2 minutes. Add the rice and stir well to coat in the mixture. Cook for 1–2 minutes.

3 Add 3–4 ladles of the hot stock to the rice mixture, stirring well to mix. Cook, stirring gently, until the liquid has almost been absorbed. Add another 3–4 ladles of the hot stock.

4 Continue cooking in this way until the mixture is thick and creamy and the rice is tender but not soft – risotto should have a little 'bite' to it. You may not need all the hot stock, just keeping adding it until the risotto is to your liking.

5 Remove from the heat. Add the butter and the diced mozzarella, stirring quickly to mix. Cover and set to one side for 5 minutes. Season with salt and freshly ground black pepper to taste.

# Nasi Goreng

This dish originates from Indonesia.

### Serves 2

**125g/4½oz long-grain rice**
**1½ tbsp sunflower oil**
**1 onion, peeled and cut into thin rings**
**1 small onion, peeled and sliced into thin wedges**
**1 clove garlic, peeled and finely chopped**
**1½ fresh, red chilli, chopped (according to taste)**
**1.25cm-/½in-piece fresh root ginger, peeled and finely grated**
**125g/4½oz carrots, peeled and coarsely grated**
**75g/3oz bean sprouts**
**½ tbsp paprika**
**1½ tbsp tomato ketchup**
**½ tbsp soy sauce**
**salt and freshly ground black pepper**
**fresh coriander, chopped, to garnish**

### Serves 4

**250g/9oz long-grain rice**
**3 tbsp sunflower oil**
**1 large onion, peeled and cut into thin rings**
**1 onion, peeled and sliced into thin wedges**
**2 cloves garlic, peeled and finely chopped**
**1–2 fresh, red chillies, chopped, (according to taste)**
**2.5cm-/1in-piece fresh root ginger, peeled and finely grated**
**250g/9oz carrots, peeled and coarsely grated**
**150g/5oz bean sprouts**
**1 tbsp paprika**
**3 tbsp tomato ketchup**
**1 tbsp soy sauce**
**salt and freshly ground black pepper**
**fresh coriander, chopped, to garnish**

1 Rinse the rice under cold running water and drain thoroughly. Now place the rice in a saucepan with 300ml/½pt (600ml/1pt) water and bring to the boil. Reduce the heat to a gentle simmer and cover with a well-fitting lid. Cook for 8–10 minutes or until all the liquid has been absorbed. Fork through to separate the rice.

Set to one side while you prepare the rest of the dish.

2 Heat the oil in a large frying pan or wok and cook the large onion over a moderately high heat until it becomes golden and crisp. Remove, using a slotted spoon, and drain on kitchen paper. Reserve for garnish.

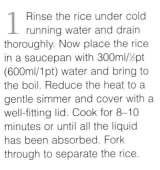

3 Cook the remaining onion in the same pan until it softens, add the garlic, chillies and ginger and continue to cook, stirring, for 2–3 minutes.

4 Now stir in the carrots, bean sprouts and paprika and stir fry for 3–4 minutes. Now add the cooked rice and mix through the vegetables thoroughly.

5 Mix the tomato ketchup and soy sauce with 1 tbsp water and then pour this over the rice mixture, stirring as you do so. Continue to cook, stirring, for 5 minutes until the mixture is piping hot. Season to taste and serve garnished with coriander and reserved onion rings.

# Lemon & Herb Risotto

*Easy Entertaining*

This thick and creamy risotto is flavoured with lemon, parsley and chives.

### Serves 2

½ tbsp olive oil
25g/1oz butter
100g/4oz onions, peeled
   and chopped
1 small clove garlic, peeled
   and crushed
300ml/½pt vegetable stock
200ml/7fl oz dry, white wine
½ lemon
150g/5 oz arborio rice
25g/1oz Parmesan cheese,
   finely grated
1½ tbsp fresh parsley,
   chopped
1 tbsp fresh chives,
   chopped
salt and freshly ground
   black pepper

### Serves 4

1 tbsp olive oil
50g/2oz butter
225g/8oz onions, peeled
   and chopped
1 clove garlic, peeled and
   crushed
600ml/1pt vegetable stock
400ml/14fl oz dry, white wine
1 lemon
300g/10½oz arborio rice
50g/2oz Parmesan cheese,
   finely grated
3 tbsp fresh parsley,
   chopped
2 tbsp fresh chives,
   chopped
salt and freshly ground
   black pepper

1 Heat the oil and half the butter in a large saucepan. Add the onions and garlic and cook over a moderate heat until they become transparent and softened. Place the stock and wine in a saucepan, heat to a very gentle simmer, cover and keep hot.

2 Finely grate the zest from the lemon and add to the rice. Squeeze the juice from the lemon and reserve.

3 Add the zest and rice to the pan stirring well to coat in the onion and garlic mixture. Cook for 1–2 minutes.

4 Now add 3–4 ladles of the hot stock to the rice mixture, stirring well to mix. Cook, stirring gently, until the liquid has almost been absorbed. Add another 3–4 ladles of the hot stock. Continue cooking in this way until the mixture is thick and creamy and the rice is tender

but not soft – risotto should have a little 'bite' to it. You may not need all the hot stock, just keeping adding it until the risotto is to your liking.

5 Remove from the heat. Add the remaining butter and the Parmesan, stirring quickly to mix. Sprinkle over the herbs and fold them through with a large metal spoon. Season with salt and freshly ground black pepper to taste and serve.

# Pad Thai

*Low Cal*

This popular Thai dish is usually made with wide rice noodles. This recipe uses egg noodles instead, and the dish tastes just as good. Pad Thai combines several different flavours, namely spicy, sour and sweet.

## Serves 2

200g/7oz flat egg noodles
½ tbsp sunflower oil
2 shallots, peeled and cut
    into wedges
1 clove garlic, peeled and
    finely chopped
2 spring onions, trimmed
    and cut into 2.5cm/1in
    lengths
1 tsp tamarind concentrate
1 tbsp soft, brown sugar
2 tbsp rice vinegar
¼ tsp dried red-chilli flakes
150g/5oz carrots, peeled
    and coarsely grated
60g/2½oz bean sprouts
3 tbsp fresh coriander,
    chopped
salt and freshly ground
    black pepper
40g/1½oz roasted peanuts,
    coarsely chopped
½ lime, cut into wedges
    (optional)

## Serves 4

400g/14oz flat egg noodles
1 tbsp sunflower oil
4 shallots, peeled and cut
    into wedges
2 cloves garlic, peeled and
    finely chopped
4 spring onions, trimmed
    and cut into 2.5cm/1in
    lengths
2 tsp tamarind concentrate
2 tbsp soft, brown sugar
4 tbsp rice vinegar
½ tsp dried red-chilli flakes
275g/10oz carrots, peeled
    and coarsely grated
150g/5oz bean sprouts
6 tbsp fresh coriander,
    chopped
salt and freshly ground
    black pepper
75g/3oz roasted peanuts,
    coarsely chopped
1 lime, cut into wedges
    (optional)

1 Cook the noodles according to the manufacturer's instructions, then drain and set to one side.

2 Heat the oil in a large frying pan or wok and cook the shallots over a moderate heat until softened.

Add the garlic and spring onions and continue to cook for a further 3–4 minutes.

3 In a small bowl mix the tamarind, sugar, vinegar and chilli flakes. Add 60ml/4 tbsp (125ml/4fl oz) of warm water, then set aside.

4 Add the carrots and bean sprouts to the pan and cook, stirring, for a further 2–3 minutes. Stir in the drained noodles along with the tamarind mixture. Increase the heat to high and stir-fry for 3–4 minutes until piping hot.

5 Stir through the chopped coriander and season to taste. Serve sprinkled with the chopped peanuts and the lime wedges if using.

# Egg-fried Rice

*Quick and Easy*

Children often love this combination of ingredients. That said, it is up to you which vegetables you add – just make sure that they are diced into quite small pieces.

## Serves 2

125g/4½oz long-grain rice
1 tbsp sunflower oil
1 onion, peeled and
    chopped
1 small clove garlic, peeled
    and crushed
125g/4½oz carrots, peeled
    and diced
50g/2oz frozen peas
50g/2oz sweet corn
1 egg
1 tbsp soy sauce
¼ tsp sesame oil
salt and freshly ground
    black pepper
1 tbsp fresh coriander,
    chopped

## Serves 4

250g/9oz long-grain rice
2 tbsp sunflower oil
1 large onion, peeled and
    chopped
1 clove garlic, peeled and
    crushed
250g/9oz carrots, peeled
    and diced
100g/4oz frozen peas
100g/4oz sweet corn
2 eggs
2 tbsp soy sauce
½ tsp sesame oil
salt and freshly ground
    black pepper
2 tbsp fresh coriander,
    chopped

1 Rinse the rice under cold running water and drain thoroughly. Place the rice in a saucepan with 300ml/½pt (600ml/1pt) water and bring to the boil. Reduce the heat to a gentle simmer and cover with a well-fitting lid. Cook for 8–10 minutes or until all the liquid has been absorbed. Set aside with the lid on while you prepare the rest of the dish.

2 In a wok or large frying pan heat the oil and cook the onion over a moderately high heat until softened. Add the garlic and carrots and continue to cook, stirring, for 5 minutes.

3 Stir in the peas and sweet corn and cook, stirring, for 1 minute. Then add the cooked rice and stir well to mix.

4 Beat the eggs, soy sauce and sesame oil together and pour over the rice mixture.

5 Increase the heat to high and cook stirring all the time until the mixture is piping hot and the egg is cooked. To serve season to taste and sprinkle with coriander.

# Spanish Rice

*One Pot*

This delicious main meal can also be served as an accompaniment – just reduce quantities by half.

### Serves 2

1½ tbsp olive oil
1 onion, peeled and finely
   chopped
1 clove garlic, peeled and
   finely chopped
½ red pepper, deseeded
   and chopped
½ green pepper, deseeded
   and chopped
75g/3oz mushrooms, sliced
½ tbsp paprika
150g/5 oz paella rice
500ml/18fl oz vegetable stock
25g/1oz almonds
salt and freshly ground
   black pepper

### Serves 4

3 tbsp olive oil
1 large onion, peeled and
   finely chopped
2 cloves garlic, peeled and
   finely chopped
1 red pepper, deseeded
   and chopped
1 green pepper, deseeded
   and chopped
150g/5oz mushrooms, sliced
1 tbsp paprika
300g/10½oz paella rice
1l/1¾pt vegetable stock
50g/2oz almonds
salt and freshly ground
   black pepper

1 In a large frying pan heat the oil and cook the onions over a moderate heat until they are softened.

2 Add the garlic, peppers and mushrooms and cook until they have changed colour and softened.

3 Sprinkle over the paprika and cook for 1–2 minutes, stirring well to mix. Stir in the rice and mix well to coat in the spiced oil mixture.

4 Now add the stock stirring well and bring to the boil. Reduce the heat to a gentle

simmer and cook, stirring from time to time, until all the liquid has been absorbed.

5 While this is cooking lightly toast the almonds under a hot grill. Watch them carefully as they will go from being nearly ready to burnt very quickly. Leave until cool enough to handle then roughly chop.

6 Season to taste and serve the rice sprinkled with the toasted almonds.

# Creamy Mushroom Pasta

*Quick and Easy*

Mascarpone is often used in Italian desserts but it works just as well in savory dishes.

## Serves 2

125g/4½oz mushrooms
200g/7oz dried pasta shapes
  (I used gigli)
1 tbsp olive oil
1 small clove garlic, peeled
  and crushed
3 spring onions, trimmed
  and finely sliced
75ml/2½fl oz dry, white wine
125g/4½oz Mascarpone
  cheese
1 tbsp fresh chives, chopped
1 tbsp fresh parsley,
  chopped
salt and freshly ground black
  pepper

## Serves 4

250g/9oz mushrooms
400g/14oz dried pasta
  shapes (I used gigli)
2 tbsp olive oil
1 clove garlic, peeled and
  crushed
6 spring onions, trimmed
  and finely sliced
150ml/¼pt dry, white wine
250g/9oz Mascarpone
  cheese
2 tbsp fresh chives, chopped
2 tbsp fresh parsley,
  chopped
salt and freshly ground black
  pepper

1 Wipe the mushrooms with a damp cloth to remove any dirt. If the mushrooms are large slice them.

2 Bring a large saucepan of water to the boil, add the pasta and cook, according to the manufacturer's instructions.

3 Heat the oil in a large frying pan and cook the garlic and spring onions for 2–3 minutes over a moderate heat. Add the mushrooms and cook for 5 minutes until the mushrooms are softened and tender.

4 Add the wine and bring it to the boil. Let the mixture boil for 2–3 minutes to reduce a little.

5 Stir in the Mascarpone, stirring well to mix. Cook for 2–3 minutes until piping hot. Remove from the heat and stir in the chopped chives and parsley. Season to taste and stir this sauce through the cooked pasta. Serve.

# Chilli & Garlic Spaghetti

*Quick and Easy*

This simple dish definitely qualifies as fast food.

### Serves 2

**150g/5oz cherry tomatoes**
**200g/7oz spaghetti pasta**
**1 tbsp olive oil**
**1 clove garlic, peeled and**
**    crushed**
**½ tsp dried red-chilli flakes**
**50g/2oz feta cheese**
**salt and freshly ground**
**    black pepper**

### Serves 4

**300g/10oz cherry tomatoes**
**400g/14oz spaghetti pasta**
**2 tbsp olive oil**
**2 cloves garlic, peeled and**
**    crushed**
**1 tsp dried red-chilli flakes**
**100g/4oz feta cheese**
**salt and freshly ground**
**    black pepper**

1 Cut the tomatoes in half and set to one side. Bring a large pan of water to the boil and cook the pasta according to the manufacturer's instructions.

2 In a frying pan heat the oil over a moderate heat, add the garlic and chilli flakes and cook, stirring, for 2 minutes.

3 Stir the tomatoes through the garlic and chilli, coating well in the oil. Remove from the heat.

4 Toss the drained spaghetti through the tomato and chilli mixture. Crumble the feta cheese over the pasta and stir lightly to mix, season to taste and serve.

# Linguine with Tomatoes & Spring Onions

*Quick and Easy*

A perfect midweek supper – cooked in minutes.

## Serves 2

200g/7oz linguine pasta
2 tomatoes
25g/1oz butter
1 small clove garlic, peeled
   and crushed
3 spring onions, trimmed
   and sliced
2 eggs
½ tbsp double cream
salt and freshly ground
   black pepper
15g/½oz Parmesan cheese,
   freshly grated

## Serves 4

400g/14oz linguine pasta
4 tomatoes
50g/2oz butter
1 clove garlic, peeled
   and crushed
6 spring onions, trimmed
   and sliced
4 eggs
1 tbsp double cream
salt and freshly ground
   black pepper
25g/1oz Parmesan cheese,
   freshly grated

1 Bring a large pan of water to the boil and cook the pasta according to the manufacturer's instructions.

2 Cut a cross in the base of each tomato and place in a bowl. Cover with boiling water. Leave for 1–2 minutes.

3 Drain. Peel, remove the seeds and discard. Cut into thin strips. Set to one side.

4 Heat the butter in a large saucepan over a moderate heat and cook the spring onions and garlic for 2–3 minutes until softened.

5 Add the tomatoes and cook for a further 3–4 minutes, stirring lightly. You don't want to break up the tomatoes too much.

6 Beat the eggs and cream together and season lightly with the salt and freshly ground black pepper.

7 Add the hot, drained linguine to the spring-onion mixture and stir well to mix. Pour over the beaten eggs and stir the mixture until the eggs have set. Sprinkle with Parmesan cheese and serve at once.

# Pepper & Potato Pasta

*Children's choice*

Potatoes and pasta may sound like an unusual combination, but don't be put off – this dish is a firm favourite with my family.

## Serves 2

175g/6oz new potatoes
2 red, yellow or orange
   peppers
1 tbsp olive oil
1 small clove garlic, peeled
   and thickly sliced
175g/6oz dried pasta shapes
1 tbsp pesto
salt and freshly ground
   black pepper
15g/½oz Parmesan cheese,
   shaved into thin slices

## Serves 4

350g/12oz new potatoes
3 large red, yellow or orange
   peppers
2 tbsp olive oil
1 clove garlic, peeled and
   thickly sliced
350g/12oz dried pasta shapes
2 tbsp pesto
salt and freshly ground
   black pepper
25g/1oz Parmesan cheese,
   shaved into thin slices

1 Wash the potatoes and cook in a large saucepan of salted boiling water until tender. This should take about 10–15 minutes. Drain thoroughly. When cool enough to handle cut into bite-size pieces.

2 Using a vegetable peeler peel as much of the skin as possible from the peppers. You won't be able to remove it all, but that doesn't matter. Removing as much as you can makes the peppers much sweeter. Now deseed the peppers and cut them into bite-size chunks.

3 Heat the oil in a large frying pan over a moderate heat and cook the garlic until it starts to turn golden. Remove, using a slotted spoon, and discard.

4 Add the peppers and stir to coat in the garlic flavoured oil. Cook, stirring from time to time, for about 15–20 minutes or until the peppers are softened and starting to turn golden in places. Remove, using a slotted spoon, and keep warm.

6

5 Add the potatoes to the pan and increase the heat a little. At this point put a large pan of water on to boil for the pasta. When the water is boiling add the pasta and cook according to the manufacturer's instructions.

6 Cook the potatoes until they become golden and crisp in places, stirring from time to time. Return the peppers to the pan and stir through to mix.

7 Drain the pasta and stir through the pesto. Add the peppers and potatoes along with any oil that is left in the pan. Toss well to mix. Season to taste and serve with the Parmesan.

salads and vegetables

# Lentil salad

*Family Favourite*

This colourful salad is good in lunch boxes or on a picnic.

## Serves 2

**175g/6oz brown lentils**
**½ small onion, peeled and**
**halved**
**½ stick celery**
**1 sprig fresh thyme**
**1 clove garlic, peeled**
**1 small bay leaf**
**1 carrot, peeled**
**½ small red onion, peeled**
**2 tbsp olive oil**
**1 tbsp white wine vinegar**
**1 tsp Dijon mustard**
**½ tsp sugar**
**salt and freshly ground**
**black pepper**
**75g/3oz feta cheese**
**3 tbsp fresh parsley,**
**chopped**

## Serves 4

**350g/12oz brown lentils**
**1 small onion, peeled and**
**halved**
**1 stick celery**
**1 large sprig fresh thyme**
**2 cloves garlic, peeled**
**1 bay leaf**
**1 large carrot, peeled**
**1 small red onion, peeled**
**4 tbsp olive oil**
**2 tbsp white wine vinegar**
**2 tsp Dijon mustard**
**1 tsp sugar**
**salt and freshly ground**
**black pepper**
**150g/5oz feta cheese**
**6 tbsp fresh parsley,**
**chopped**

1 Place the lentils in a colander and wash thoroughly under cold running water. Drain.

2 Place them in a large saucepan with the halved onion, celery, thyme, garlic and bay leaf. Cover with plenty of cold water and bring to the boil. Reduce the heat to a gentle simmer and cook for 30 minutes until they are tender. Drain and leave to cool. Now discard the onion, celery, thyme, garlic and bay leaf.

3 Coarsely grate the carrot into a large mixing bowl. Finely slice the red onion and add to the carrot. Add the cooled lentils and toss to mix.

4 In a small bowl whisk the olive oil with the vinegar mustard and sugar, season to taste. Now pour the vinaigrette over the lentil mixture and toss to mix.

5 To serve crumble the feta cheese and add to the salad along with the chopped parsley. Toss and adjust seasoning as necessary.

# Roasted Carrots

*Easy Entertaining*

This recipe may seem to specify a lot of carrots, but be reassured that they reduce quite a lot in size as they roast.

## Serves 2

**500g/1lb 2oz carrots, peeled and cut into batons**
**2 tbsp olive oil**
**1½ tbsp fresh thyme, roughly chopped**
**1 tbsp cider vinegar**
**salt and freshly ground black pepper**

## Serves 4

**1kg/2¼lb carrots, peeled and cut into batons**
**4 tbsp olive oil**
**3 tbsp fresh thyme, roughly chopped**
**2 tbsp cider vinegar**
**salt and freshly ground black pepper**

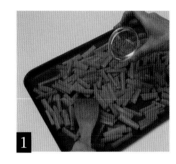

1 Preheat the oven to 200°C/400°F/Gas 6. Place the carrots in a large shallow roasting tin. Drizzle over the olive oil and toss well to coat the carrots.

2 Roast in the preheated oven for 20 minutes. Now add the chopped thyme and toss again to mix. Return to the oven and cook for a further 15 minutes.

3 Add the vinegar and stir then return to the oven for 10 minutes.

4 To serve place in a dish and season to taste.

# Carrot & Courgette Timbales

*Easy Entertaining*

These timbales are really quick and easy to prepare.

## Serves 2

175g/6oz carrots, peeled
175g/6oz courgettes,
    trimmed
½ tbsp olive oil
1 small clove garlic, peeled
    and crushed
1½ tbsp fresh chives,
    chopped
½ tbsp fresh parsley,
    chopped
salt and freshly ground
    black pepper

## Serves 4

350g/12oz carrots, peeled
350g/12oz courgettes,
    trimmed
1 tbsp olive oil
1 clove garlic, peeled and
    crushed
3 tbsp fresh chives,
    chopped
1 tbsp fresh parsley,
    chopped
salt and freshly ground
    black pepper

1 Coarsely grate the carrots and courgettes and mix.

2 Heat the oil and garlic over a moderate heat for 1–2 minutes until the oil is hot and the garlic is starting to sizzle. Do not let the garlic brown too much or the mixture will taste bitter.

3 Now add the grated carrots and courgettes and toss quickly to mix. Increase the heat to high and cover the pan with a well-fitting lid.

4 Cook covered, shaking the pan from time to time, for 5 minutes. Remove from the heat and stir through the chopped herbs. Season with salt and freshly ground black pepper.

5 Pile the mixture into a small mould or pudding basin, pressing down with the back of a spoon to level, Turn out onto a plate to serve. Repeat with the remaining mixture until you have 2 (4) portions.

# New Potatoes in Red Wine & Rosemary

*Easy Entertaining*

Adding red wine and herbs to new potatoes makes them a bit more special.

## Serves 2

½ tbsp olive oil
15g/½oz butter
2 shallots, peeled and
    chopped
250g/9oz small new potatoes,
    scrubbed
½ tbsp fresh thyme, chopped
½ tbsp fresh rosemary,
    chopped
150ml/¼pt red wine
salt and freshly ground
    black pepper

## Serves 4

1 tbsp olive oil
25g/1oz butter
4 shallots, peeled and
    chopped
500g/1lb 1oz small new
    potatoes, scrubbed
1 tbsp fresh thyme, chopped
1 tbsp fresh rosemary,
    chopped
300ml/½pt red wine
salt and freshly ground
    black pepper

1 Heat the olive oil and butter in a large frying pan that has a lid. Cook the chopped shallots over a moderate heat until they are softened.

2 Add the potatoes and increase the heat a little. Cook, stirring from time to time, until the potatoes start to turn golden in places.

3 Stir in the chopped herbs and cook for 2–3 minutes. Now pour over the wine and bring to the boil. Reduce the heat to a gentle simmer and cook, covered, for 15 minutes until the potatoes are tender and the wine has reduced a little.

4 Using a fork slightly crush the potatoes, season to taste and serve with some of the herb-flavoured wine spooned over.

# Salad of Green Beans

*Children's Choice*

This is one of those dishes that I never serve as an appetiser, yet whenever I make it, it seems as though no one can walk by without having a taste! Note that the green beans must be young and fresh if this recipe is to work well.

## Serves 4

**500g/1lb1oz fine green beans**
**3 tbsp olive oil**
**1 tbsp white wine vinegar**
**1 clove garlic, peeled and crushed**
**1 tsp Dijon mustard**
**a pinch of sugar**
**finely grated zest of 1 lemon**
**50g/2oz toasted almonds**
**Salt and freshly ground black pepper to taste**

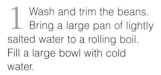

1 Wash and trim the beans. Bring a large pan of lightly salted water to a rolling boil. Fill a large bowl with cold water.

2 Blanch the beans in the boiling water for about 2 minutes. When they turn bright green, they have cooked for long enough.

3 Remove the beans, using a slotted spoon, and plunge them into the cold water. Leave in the cold water for 2–3 minutes. Drain and place in a serving bowl or on a plate.

4 In a small mixing bowl whisk the oil and vinegar together. Add the garlic, mustard and sugar and whisk again.

5 Season to taste with salt and freshly ground black pepper. Stir in the lemon zest.

6 Drizzle the dressing over the beans. Roughly chop the toasted almonds and serve at room temperature.

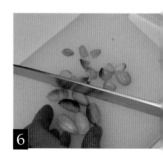

# Lemon & Garlic-buttered Peas

*Quick and Easy*

This trio of peas makes a lovely, bright-looking accompaniment to any main meal.

## Serves 2

1 shallot
15g/½oz butter
100g/4oz sugar snaps
100g/4oz mangetout
100g/4oz frozen peas
1 small clove garlic, peeled
   and crushed
½ lemon
salt and freshly ground
   black pepper

## Serves 4

2 shallots
25g/1oz butter
200g/7oz sugar snaps
200g/7oz mangetout
200g/7oz frozen peas
1 clove garlic, peeled and
   crushed
1 lemon
salt and freshly ground
   black pepper

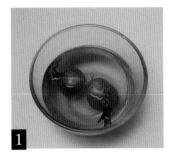

1 Place the shallots in a mixing bowl and cover with boiling water. Set to one side for 5–10 minutes. Drain and peel, then finely chop.

2 Melt the butter in a large saucepan and cook the shallots over a gentle heat.

3 Bring a large pan of water to the boil and cook the sugar snaps, mange tout and peas for 2–3 minutes until hot and tender. The mange tout and sugar snaps should still be slightly crisp. Drain.

4 Add the garlic to the shallots and cook for 1 minute, stirring to mix. Add the cooked peas and stir to coat in the buttery juices.

5 Finely grate the zest from the lemon and toss through the peas. Squeeze 1 (2) tbsp of juice from the lemon and stir into the peas along with seasoning to taste. Serve.

# Potato Salad

*Children's Choice*

Potato salads are so versatile, and the combination of ingredients that can be included in them is almost endless. I like to add some Greek yoghurt to the mayonnaise to give it a bit of bite, having found that too much mayonnaise tastes a little cloying.

## Serves 2

**250g/9oz baby new potatoes**
**1 small, crisp eating apple**
**2 sticks celery**
**2 spring onions, trimmed**
**50g/2oz cornichons, drained**
**1 tbsp fresh parsley,**
   **chopped**
**1½ tbsp mayonnaise**
**1 tbsp Greek yoghurt**
**salt and freshly ground**
   **black pepper**

## Serves 4

**500g/1lb 2oz baby new**
   **potatoes**
**1 large, crisp eating apple**
**4 sticks celery**
**4 spring onions, trimmed**
**100g/4oz cornichons, drained**
**1 tbsp fresh parsley,**
   **chopped**
**3 tbsp mayonnaise**
**2 tbsp Greek yoghurt**
**salt and freshly ground**
   **black pepper**

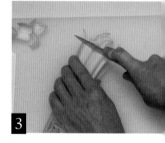

1 Cook the potatoes in a large pan of lightly salted boiling water for approximately 10 minutes until tender. Drain and set to one side to cool.

2 Cut the apple into quarters and remove the core. Cut into bite-size pieces and place in a large mixing bowl.

3 Trim and slice the celery and add to the apple. Finely slice the spring onions and cornichons and add to the bowl. Toss to mix.

4 In a small bowl mix the chopped parsley with the mayonnaise and Greek yoghurt. Season with salt and freshly ground black pepper to taste.

5 Toss the seasoned mayonnaise through the apple mixture. Finally add the cooled potatoes and stir lightly to mix. Serve.

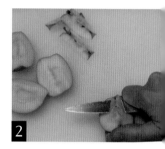

# Satay Noodles

*Children's Choice*

Quick and easy, this dish is also good cold.

## Serves 2

100g/4oz egg noodles
½ tbsp sesame oil
1½ heaped tbsp crunchy
    peanut butter
½ tbsp rice vinegar
½ tbsp soft, brown sugar
1.25cm-/½in-piece fresh root
    ginger, peeled and grated
1 small clove garlic, peeled
    and crushed
½ tsp tamarind concentrate
½ tbsp sweet chilli sauce
50ml/3½ tbsp vegetable stock
75g/3oz tofu
½ tbsp sunflower oil
125g/4½oz carrots, peeled
    and grated
3 spring onions, trimmed
1 tbsp fresh coriander,
    chopped
salt and freshly ground
    black pepper

## Serves 4

200g/7oz egg noodles
1 tbsp sesame oil
3 heaped tbsp crunchy
    peanut butter
1 tbsp rice vinegar
1 tbsp soft, brown sugar
2.5cm-/1in-piece fresh root
    ginger, peeled and grated
1 clove garlic, peeled and
    crushed
1 tsp tamarind concentrate
1 tbsp sweet chilli sauce
100ml/3½fl oz vegetable stock
150g/5oz tofu
1 tbsp sunflower oil
250g/9oz carrots, peeled and
    grated
6 spring onions, trimmed
2 tbsp fresh coriander,
    chopped
salt and freshly ground
    black pepper

1 Cook the noodles following the manufacturer's instructions. Drain. Toss with the sesame oil.

2 Mix together the peanut butter, vinegar, sugar, ginger, garlic, tamarind and chilli sauce. Stir in the stock and mix well. Pour over the noodles and toss well to mix.

3 Drain the tofu and pat dry with kitchen paper. Cut into small pieces with a sharp knife.

Heat the oil in a frying pan over a moderate heat and cook the tofu, turning from time to time until golden. Remove, using a slotted spoon, and drain on kitchen paper.

4 Add the carrots to the noodles. Thinly slice the spring onions on the diagonal. Add to the noodles and toss again to mix.

5 Lightly mix in the coriander and tofu. Season to taste.

# Balsamic Onions, Mushrooms & Tomatoes with Rice

*Easy Entertaining*

The balsamic vinegar really complements all the ingredients in this dish.

## Serves 2

1 large onion, peeled and
    cut into wedges
2 tbsp olive oil
75g/3oz cherry tomatoes
75g/3oz button mushrooms
1 tbsp fresh rosemary,
    chopped
1 small clove garlic, peeled
    and crushed
1 tbsp balsamic vinegar
75g/3oz basmati rice
salt and freshly ground
    black pepper

## Serves 4

2 large onions, peeled and
    cut into wedges
4 tbsp olive oil
150g/5oz cherry tomatoes
150g/5oz button mushrooms
2 tbsp fresh rosemary,
    chopped
1 clove garlic, peeled and
    crushed
2 tbsp balsamic vinegar
150g/5oz basmati rice
salt and freshly ground
    black pepper

1 Preheat the oven to 200°C/ 400°F/Gas 6. Place the onions and oil in a roasting tin and toss the onions to coat in the oil. Roast in the preheated oven for 20 minutes.

2 Add the cherry tomatoes, mushrooms, rosemary and garlic, tossing well to mix. Return the tin to the oven for 10 minutes.

3 Pour over the balsamic vinegar and toss gently. Cook for a further 5 minutes. Then remove and set aside.

4 Place the rice in a saucepan with 300ml/½pt (600ml/1pt) water and bring to the boil. Reduce the heat to a gentle simmer and cover with a well-fitting lid. Cook for 8–10 minutes or until all the liquid has been absorbed. Remove from the heat and fork through to separate the rice.

5 Add the contents of the roasting tin to the rice and mix gently. Season to taste and serve.

# Coleslaw with Croutons

*Quick and Easy*

This dish tastes nothing like the coleslaw that is sold in tubs in supermarkets.

## Serves 2

40g/1½oz wholemeal bread
15g/½oz Parmesan cheese, finely grated
25g/1oz mature Cheddar cheese, grated
25g/1oz walnuts, roughly chopped
2 tbsp olive oil
1 small clove garlic, peeled and crushed
½ tbsp balsamic vinegar
½ tsp Dijon mustard
¼ tsp caster sugar
salt and freshly ground black pepper
175g/6oz white cabbage
125g/4½oz carrots, peeled
½ small, red onion, peeled

## Serves 4

75g/3oz wholemeal bread
25g/1oz Parmesan cheese, finely grated
50g/2oz mature Cheddar cheese, grated
50g/2oz walnuts, roughly chopped
4 tbsp olive oil
1 clove garlic, peeled and crushed
1 tbsp balsamic vinegar
1 tsp Dijon mustard
½ tsp caster sugar
salt and freshly ground black pepper
350g/12oz white cabbage
250g/9oz carrots, peeled
1 small, red onion, peeled

1

2

3

1 Preheat the oven to 200°C/400°F/Gas 6. Cut the bread into small cubes and spread in a single layer over a lightly greased baking tray. Mix the cheeses and chopped walnuts together. Sprinkle over the bread.

2 Bake in the preheated oven for 10–15 minutes until the cheese is melted and the bread is crisp. Allow to cool then break into bite-size chunks.

3 Place the olive oil, crushed garlic, vinegar, mustard and sugar in a mixing bowl and whisk until mixed. Season to taste.

4 Finely shred the white cabbage and place in a large serving bowl. Coarsely grate the carrot and add. Finely slice the red onion and add. Toss well to mix.

5 Pour the dressing over the cabbage mixture and toss again. Serve with the croutons sprinkled over.

# Chef's Salad

*Quick and Easy*

Children often love to help put this salad together, arranging the ingredients.

### Serves 2

**2 eggs**
**100g/4oz green beans, trimmed**
**75g/3oz hard cheese of your choice**
**100g/4oz cherry tomatoes**
**1 cos lettuce, washed and drained**
**50g/2oz black olives**
**25g/1oz pine nuts, toasted**
**2 tbsp French dressing**

### Serves 4

**4 eggs**
**225g/8oz green beans, trimmed**
**175g/6oz hard cheese of your choice**
**200g/7oz cherry tomatoes**
**2 cos lettuces, washed and drained**
**100g/4oz black olives**
**50g/2oz pine nuts, toasted**
**4 tbsp French dressing**

1 Place the eggs in a pan and cover with cold water. Bring to the boil and simmer for 10 minutes. Remove from the heat. Drain the water, cover the eggs with cold water and leave to cool.

2 Bring a saucepan of water to the boil. Add the green beans and cook for 2–3 minutes. Drain and then plunge the beans in cold water to cool.

3 Cut the cheese into thin strips and set to one side. Peel the eggs and quarter. Halve the cherry tomatoes

4 Tear the lettuce into bite-size pieces and arrange on a serving plate. Now arrange the beans, cheese, eggs and tomatoes over the lettuce. Scatter over the olives and pine nuts. Serve drizzled with dressing.

# Green Couscous

Easy Entertaining

Packed full of fresh herbs, this salad is really refreshing.

### Serves 2

**125g/4½oz couscous**
**½ vegetable stock cube**
**5cm-/2in-piece cucumber**
**1 large tomato**
**25g/1oz fresh mint**
**25g/1oz fresh parsley**
**1 tbsp olive oil**
**1 tsp lemon juice**
**salt and freshly ground**
**   black pepper**

### Serves 4

**250g/9oz couscous**
**1 vegetable stock cube**
**10cm-/4in-piece cucumber**
**2 large tomatoes**
**40g/1½oz fresh mint**
**40g/1½oz fresh parsley**
**2 tbsp olive oil**
**2 tsp lemon juice**
**salt and freshly ground**
**   black pepper**

1 Place the couscous in a large bowl. Dissolve the stock cube in 150ml/¼pt (300ml/½pt) boiling water then pour over the couscous and stir once. Cover with cling film and set to one side to soak for 10–15 minutes.

2 Halve the cucumber. Use a teaspoon to remove the seeds from the cucumber and discard. Now cut the flesh into fine dice.

3 Remove the seeds from the tomatoes and discard. Cut the flesh into fine dice.

4 Remove all the stalks from the mint and parsley and then finely chop.

5 Add the olive oil and lemon juice to the couscous along with the tomatoes and cucumbers and fork through. Season to taste and serve.

# Chinese Salad

*Children's choice*

Bright and colourful with lots of crunch.

## Serves 2

**100g/4oz baby corn**
**75g/3oz mangetout**
**1 red pepper**
**75g/3oz bean sprouts**
**1 small egg**
**1 tsp sesame oil**
**1 tbsp soy sauce**
**½ tbsp sesame seeds**
**1 tbsp sunflower oil**
**½ tbsp honey**
**1.25cm-/½in-piece fresh root**
**    ginger, peeled and finely**
**    grated**
**1 small clove garlic, peeled**
**    and crushed**
**½ tbsp lemon juice**

## Serves 4

**200g/7oz baby corn**
**150g/5oz mangetout**
**1 large red pepper**
**150g/5oz bean sprouts**
**1 large egg**
**2 tsp sesame oil**
**2 tbsp soy sauce**
**1 tbsp sesame seeds**
**2 tbsp sunflower oil**
**1 tbsp honey**
**2.5cm-/1in-piece fresh root**
**    ginger, peeled and finely**
**    grated**
**1 clove garlic, peeled and**
**    crushed**
**1 tbsp lemon juice**

1 Cut the baby corn in half if large. Trim the tops from the mangetout and halve.

2 Bring a pan of water to the boil. Add the corn and bring back to boil. Cook for 2 minutes. Add the mangetout and cook for a further minute at a rolling boil. Remove from the boiling water, using a slotted spoon, and plunge the vegetables straight into a bowl of cold water.

3 Deseed the pepper and cut into thin strips. Place in a large bowl, and add the bean sprouts.

4 In a bowl beat the egg together with the sesame oil, half the soy sauce and 1 tbsp of water. Lightly oil a non-stick frying pan over a moderately high heat and pour in just enough of the beaten egg mixture to cover the base of the pan. Sprinkle over some of the sesame seeds and cook for 1–2 minutes or until set. Turn over and cook for a further minute. then Remove and set to one side. Repeat with the remaining mixture until you have used it all.

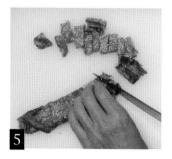

5

5 Roll the sesame omelettes up. Use a sharp knife to cut into thin slices.

6 Drain the baby corn and mangetout and add to the peppers and bean sprouts.

7 Mix the remaining soy sauce, sunflower oil, honey, ginger, garlic and lemon juice together. Pour this mixture over the vegetables and toss well to mix. Serve scattered with the sesame omelette rolls.

# sweet
# things

# Three-fruit Crumble

*Easy Entertaining*

Crumbles are so delicious and they are easy to make. Don't be tempted to make the crumble mixture in a food processor as you risk losing the rough texture that gives the lovely crunch and crumble.

### Serves 4-6

**175g/6oz self-raising flour**
**75g/3oz butter**
**25g/1oz ground almonds**
**100g/4oz demerara sugar**
**550/1lb 3oz cooking apples**
**500g/1lb 2oz ripe pears**
**400/14oz plums**
**2–3 tbsp sugar, or according to taste**
**50g/2oz flaked almonds**

1 Preheat the oven to 350°F/180°C/Gas 4. Sift the flour into a mixing bowl, add the butter and rub it in using your fingertips. When the mixture resembles coarse breadcrumbs stir through the ground almonds and demerara sugar. Set to one side while you make the rest of the dish.

2 Peel and core the apples and pears. Cut into thin slices and place in a baking dish. Cut the plums in half and remove the stones. Add the plums to the apples and pears and sprinkle over the sugar.

3 Top evenly with the crumble mixture but do not press it into place. Place in the preheated oven and bake for 25 minutes.

4 Sprinkle the flaked almonds over the top of the crumble and return to the oven for a further 10–15 minutes until golden and crisp in places. Serve hot with custard or cream.

# Citrus Crème Brûlée

*Easy Entertaining*

The combination of orange-flavoured creamy custard and a dark, crisp, sugary top, always seems to please.

## Serves 2

**40g/1½oz caster sugar**
**finely grated zest of ½ orange**
**2 egg yolks**
**200ml/7fl oz single cream**
**approx. 1½ tbsp demerara**
    **sugar**

## Serves 4

**75g/3oz caster sugar**
**finely grated zest of 1 orange**
**4 egg yolks**
**400ml/14fl oz single cream**
**approx. 3 tbsp demerara**
    **sugar**

1 Preheat the oven to 150°C/300°F/Gas 2. Place the caster sugar in a bowl. Add the finely grated orange zest and mix. Add the egg yolks and beat well with a wooden spoon until well mixed.

2 Heat the cream gently until almost boiling. Remove from the heat and pour in a steady stream over the egg yolks, stirring all the time until fully combined.

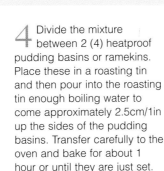

3 Return this mixture to the pan and cook gently, stirring with a wooden spoon, until the mixture thickens. The best way to test this is by running your finger over the back of the wooden spoon. If it leaves a clean trail then it is thickened.

4 Divide the mixture between 2 (4) heatproof pudding basins or ramekins. Place these in a roasting tin and then pour into the roasting tin enough boiling water to come approximately 2.5cm/1in up the sides of the pudding basins. Transfer carefully to the oven and bake for about 1 hour or until they are just set. Remove from the oven and allow to cool fully. Place in the fridge to chill.

5 About 30 minutes before serving preheat the grill to high and sprinkle the tops of each crème with a thin even layer of demerara sugar. Place under the grill and cook, turning if necessary, until all the sugar has melted. Remove from the heat and set to one side to cool fully before serving.

# Toffee-apple Tart

*Easy Entertaining*

With its creamy caramel and slightly tart apple on crisp, buttery pastry, this is the sort of tart that you won't be able to resist having another sliver of!

## Serves 6-8

**250g/9oz plain flour**
**150g/5oz unsalted butter, roughly chopped and chilled**
**250g/9oz dulche de lait**
**2 tbsp apricot jam**
**1 tbsp lemon juice**
**3–4 eating apples**

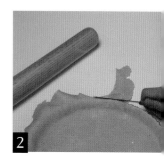

1 Place the flour and butter in the bowl of a food processor and pulse until the mixture resembles coarse breadcrumbs. Add 3 tbsp chilled water and pulse briefly. Remove from the machine and bring together to form a dough. If you need to add a little extra water do so almost a tsp at a time. If you add too much water you risk making the pastry tough. Wrap in cling film and place in the fridge to chill for 30 minutes.

2 Roll the pastry out on a lightly floured surface and use to line a 23cm/9in fluted tart tin. Return to the fridge while you preheat the oven to 200°C/400°F/Gas 6.

3 Line the pastry case with greaseproof paper and fill with baking beans. Bake blind for 15 minutes. Remove the baking beans and greaseproof paper and cook the pastry for a further 5 minutes.

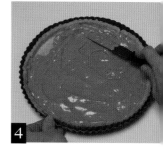

4 Spread the dulche de lait over the base of the pastry case. Heat the jam and lemon juice together and keep warm while you prepare the apples.

5 Peel and core the apples. Slice thinly and arrange over the dulche de lait.

6 Brush the top with the lemon juice and jam. Place in the preheated oven for 25 minutes until piping hot and golden in places. Leave to cool for 15 minutes before serving. Can also be served at room temperature.

# Caramelised-banana & Coffee Cake

*Children's Choice*

If you don't have time to make the caramel-cream filling for this cake, you could always fill it with plain, whipped cream, or even with vanilla-butter icing. If you like, lightly dust the top of the cake with icing sugar before serving it.

*Serves 6-8*

| | |
|---|---|
| 175g/6oz butter, plus extra for greasing | 225g/8oz caster sugar |
| 50g/2oz demerara sugar | 3 eggs |
| 2 small, ripe bananas | 2 tsp strong, black coffee |
| 1 tbsp, plus 1 tsp, lemon juice | 175g/6oz self-raising flour |
| | 150ml/¼pt double cream |

1 Grease and base line 2 x18cm/7in sandwich tins. Preheat the oven to 190°C/375°F/Gas 5. Grease the base liberally with butter. Sprinkle with the demerara sugar. Slice the banana and arrange over the sugar. Sprinkle over 1 tbsp of lemon juice. Set to one side.

2 In a mixing bowl beat the butter with 175g/6oz caster sugar until light and fluffy. Beat the eggs and coffee together. Add to the butter mixture a little at a time, beating well between each addition. If the mixture starts to look curdled add a little sifted flour. Fold in the flour. Divide the mixture between the tins, levelling over the sliced bananas. Bake in the

preheated oven for 25–30 minutes until risen and springy to the touch. Remove from the oven and cool in the tin for 10 minutes. Turn out onto a wire rack and leave to cool fully.

3 Place the remaining caster sugar in a small heavy-based pan and heat gently, stirring from time to time, until melted. Continue to cook the sugar without stirring until it starts to caramelise. Remove from the heat and quickly add the remaining lemon juice and 4 tbsp of cream and mix. Cool for 10 minutes. Whip the remaining cream in a mixing bowl until it stands in soft peaks. Fold in the cooled caramel mix. Use to sandwich the cakes together.

# Choc-orange Bars

*Family Favourite*

Children love making these choc-orange bars.

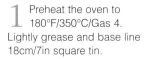

*Makes 8 bars*

**100g/4oz butter**
**175g/6oz dark chocolate**
**100g/4oz self-raising flour**
**15g/½oz cocoa powder**
**50g/2oz caster sugar**
**75g/3oz rolled oats**
**2 tbsp double cream**
**1 orange**

1 Preheat the oven to 180°F/350°C/Gas 4. Lightly grease and base line 18cm/7in square tin.

2 Dice the butter and place in a heatproof bowl. Chop 75g/3oz of the chocolate into small pieces and add to the butter. Place the bowl over a pan of gently simmering water, ensuring that the base of the bowl is not in contact with the water. Stir from time to time until melted and well mixed.

3 Sift the flour and cocoa into a mixing bowl. Add the caster sugar and oats. Stir to mix. Add the melted chocolate and butter mixture, stirring well to mix.

4 Press the mixture into the prepared tin. Bake in the preheated oven for 25 minutes. Allow to cool for 15 minutes.

5 Chop the remaining chocolate and place in a heatproof bowl along with the cream. Bring a pan of water to the boil and remove from the heat. Set the bowl over the hot water, ensuring the base of the bowl is not in contact with the water. Stir from time to time until melted.

6 Finely grate the zest from the orange. Stir into the melted chocolate mixture. Set aside to cool a little before spreading over the cooled mixture in the tin. Leave to cool fully. Use a sharp knife to cut into bars. Store in an airtight container.

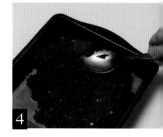

# Fresh Orange Tart

*Family Favourite*

Crisp, sweet pastry topped with creamy, vanilla-flavoured custard and finished with a slice of tart orange – delicious!

## Serves 6-8

1 large, or 2 small, thin-
    skinned oranges, washed
100g/4oz granulated sugar
150g/5oz plain flour
75g/3oz butter, diced &
    chilled

125g/4oz caster sugar
1 egg, plus 2 yolks
450ml/¾pt full-cream milk
4 tbsp cornflour
1 tsp vanilla essence

1 Slice oranges thinly. Heat 300ml/½pt water in a saucepan with the granulated sugar. Stir until the sugar has dissolved. Add the orange slices. Simmer for 30 minutes. Lay the slices on a sheet of baking parchment.

2 In a mixing bowl sift the flour. Add the butter and rub in until it resembles coarse breadcrumbs. Stir in 50g/2oz of the caster sugar and mix. Beat the whole egg and add. Stir until the mixture starts to form a dough. With lightly floured hands bring the mixture together and knead briefly.

3 Roll out on a lightly floured surface and use to line a 35 x 11cm/14 x 4½in oblong, loose-bottom tart tin. Chill for 20 minutes. Preheat the oven to 190°C/375°F/Gas 5 and place a heavy gauge baking tray in the oven to heat.

4 Line the pastry with greaseproof paper and fill with baking beans. Place on the preheated baking tray and cook for 20 minutes. Remove the paper and beans. Return to the oven for 5 minutes until the base is cooked and looks crisp. Leave in the tin and stand on a wire rack to cool.

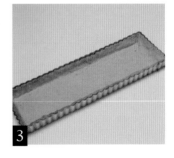

5 Heat the milk in a saucepan until almost boiling. In a mixing basin beat the egg yolk, the remaining caster sugar, cornflour and vanilla essence with 2–3 tbsp of milk until smooth. Pour over the rest of the milk in a steady stream, stirring all the time. Return the mixture to the pan and cook, stirring, until thickened. Remove and cool fully. Occasionally stir to prevent a skin forming. When cold spoon the custard into the pastry case and level. Arrange the orange slices on top.

# Boozy Apple Pie

*Family Favourite*

This apple pie tastes just as good hot or cold, or when served with cream or custard. Although I've used Calvados (an apple brandy), the type of liqueur is up to you. If you prefer, you could omit the alcohol and instead use the same quantity of single cream.

## Serves 6-8

**225g/8oz plain flour**
**175g/6oz unsalted butter, chilled and diced**
**5 tbsp caster sugar**
**3 eggs**
**700g/1lb 8oz Granny Smith apples**
**2 tbsp single cream**
**4 tbsp Calvados (or a liqueur of your choice)**

1 Sift the flour into a large mixing bowl and add 125g/4½oz of the chilled butter. Rub the butter into the flour until it resembles coarse breadcrumbs. Stir in 2 tbsp of the sugar. Beat one of the eggs with 2 tbsp cold water. Using a knife stir into the flour mixture to form a dough. Bring the dough together with your hands. Place in fridge to chill for 30 minutes.

2 Preheat the oven to 200°C/400°F/Gas 6. Roll out the pastry on a lightly floured surface and use to line a 23cm/9in fluted tart tin. Return to the fridge to chill.

3 To prepare the filling, peel, core and dice the apples and place in a large mixing bowl.

4 Melt the remaining butter and stir in the sugar. Remove from the heat and add the cream and the brandy.

5 Beat the egg and stir in. Pour this mixture over the prepared apples and toss to mix. Pour into the prepared pastry case and bake in the preheated oven for 25–30 minutes, until set and golden in places. Serve hot or cold with cream or custard.

# Chocolate & Vanilla Tarts

A lovely teatime treat.

### Serves 4

**300g/10oz sweet, shortcrust pastry**
**100g/4oz dark chocolate**
**150g/5oz Mascarpone cheese**
**3 tbsp double cream**
**2 tbsp icing sugar, sifted**
**1 tsp vanilla essence**

1 On a lightly floured surface roll the pastry out in a rough circle to a thickness of 5mm/¼in. Use to line 2 (4) 10cm/4in individual tart tins. Chill for 30 minutes.

2 Pre heat the oven to 190°C/375°F/Gas 5 and place a baking sheet in the oven to heat. Break the chocolate into a small heat-proof bowl and set over a pan of very gently simmering water. Melt the chocolate, stirring from time to time. Once the chocolate has melted remove from the heat and allow to cool a little. Now stir in 50g/2oz (100g/4oz) of the Mascarpone. Mix until fully combined.

3 Line the pastry cases with squares of greaseproof paper and baking beans.

Place on the preheated baking sheet and bake in the preheated oven for 10 minutes. Remove the greaseproof paper and baking beans. Lightly prick the base of each tart with a fork. Return to the oven for a further 5–10minutes or until the pastry is golden and crisp. Set to one side to cool.

4 Beat the remaining Mascarpone with the cream, icing sugar and vanilla essence until smooth.

5 When the pastry cases are fully cooled divide the chocolate mixture between them. Dot small spoonfuls of the vanilla mixture over the chocolate and then ripple by dragging a skewer or knife tip through the mixture. Chill until ready to serve.

# Chocolate & Cream Liqueur Brownies

*Family Favourite*

Rich and chocolaty, delicious as they are or served warm with ice cream.

## Makes 8

**175g/6oz butter or margarine**
**175g/6oz dark chocolate, chopped**
**3 eggs**
**90ml/3fl oz cream liqueur**
**75g/3oz plain flour, sifted**
**50g/2oz cocoa powder, sifted**
**175g/6oz caster sugar**

1 Preheat the oven to 180°C/350°F/Gas 4. Grease and base line a 18cm/7in baking tin.

2 Place the butter and chocolate in a mixing bowl over a pan of gently simmering water, ensuring that the base of the bowl is not in contact with the water. Stir from time to time until the chocolate and butter are melted.

3 Remove from the heat and beat the eggs in one at a time. Beat well between each addition.

4 Stir in the cream liqueur. Add the sifted flour and cocoa and mix. Finally stir in the caster sugar. Pour the mixture into the prepared tin and bake in the preheated oven for 20–25 minutes until the mixture is just set. Remove from the oven and set the tin on a wire rack. Leave until cold. Cut into squares and serve.

# Nutty Flapjacks

*Children's Choice*

Delicious and healthy treats!

*makes 9*

**100g/4oz butter or margarine**
**50g/2oz light-brown sugar**
**4 tbsp runny honey**
**175g/6oz rolled oats**
**2 tbsp plain flour**
**50g/2oz pecan nuts, roughly chopped**
**50g/2oz hazelnuts, roughly chopped**

1 Preheat the oven to 190°C/375°F/Gas 5. Grease and base line 20cm/8in square baking tin.

2 In a large saucepan heat the butter over a moderate heat until melted. Add the sugar and honey and stir until the sugar has dissolved.

3 Remove from the heat and stir in the oats and flour, mixing well to combine.

4 Stir through the nuts. Press the mixture into the prepared tin, levelling the top with the back of a spoon. Bake in the preheated oven for 25–30 minutes until golden and firm. Remove from the oven and set on a wire rack for 5 minutes.

5 Mark into squares with a knife and then leave to cool fully before removing from the tin. Store in an airtight container.

# Lemon & Ginger Buns

*Quick and Easy*

These buns make a handy, wholesome snack for any time of the day.

## Makes 8

**175g/6oz wholemeal flour**
**1½ tsp baking powder**
**1 tsp ground ginger**
**75g/3oz butter or margarine**
**75g/3oz soft, light-brown sugar**
**25g/1oz chopped, mixed peel**
**1 lemon**
**100g/4oz dried, ready-to-eat apricots, chopped**
**1 egg**

1 Preheat the oven to 220°C/425°F/Gas 7. Lightly grease a large baking tray.

2 Place the flour, baking powder and ginger in a bowl and mix. Add the butter and cut into pieces. Rub in the butter until the mixture resembles coarse breadcrumbs.

3 Stir in the sugar and mixed peel. Finely grate the zest from the lemon and add, stirring well to mix.

4 Stir in the chopped apricots. Beat the egg and add to the mixture along with enough lemon juice to make a stiff dough.

5 Place heaped spoonfuls on the prepared baking tray, leaving space between each one to allow for rising. Bake in the preheated oven for 15 minutes until golden and risen. Cool on a wire rack before storing in an airtight container.

# index

## A

## B

## C

## D

## E

## F

## G

## H

## L

## M

# credits & acknowledgements

Thanks to Harrison Fisher and Co (www.premiercutlery.co.uk) for supplying the knives and some of the small kitchen utensils used for the step-by-step pictures. Also thanks to Magimix whose food processor has well and truly earned its place on my kitchen worktop, making light work of the soups and some of the other dishes in this book. And thanks to Braun for the Multiquick, which was invaluable in preparing so many of the recipes.

I would also like to thank my family and Colin Bowling for all their interest, support and encouragement.